Adi Mazen Adi is a Human Resources expert with more than 14 years of professional experience. His passion is to enhance the organisational performance through deploying a proven and successfully applied HR best practices.

Adi is a professional HR certifications instructor and has contributed to the development of many HR professionals. He has written many articles on both SHRM website and LinkedIn. He has established the first SHRM forum in Jordan in order to help advance the HR profession within his community.

For all who inspired me to write this book with love.

Adi Mazen Adi

The Four Levels of HR Excellence

Mastering the Basic HR Functions and Measuring Their Effectiveness

AUSTIN MACAULEY PUBLISHERS™

LONDON * CAMBRIDGE * NEW YORK * SHARJAH

Copyright © Adi Mazen Adi (2021)

The right of Adi Mazen Adi to be identified as author of this work has been asserted by the author in accordance with Federal Law No. (7) of UAE, Year 2002, Concerning Copyrights and Neighbouring Rights.

All rights reserved. No part of this publication may be reproduced, stored in a retrieval system, or transmitted in any form or by any means; electronic, mechanical, photocopying, recording, or otherwise, without the prior permission of the publishers.

Any person who commits any unauthorised act in relation to this publication may be liable to legal prosecution and civil claims for damages.

The age category suitable for the books' contents has been classified and defined in accordance to the Age Classification System issued by the National Media Council.

ISBN – 9789948452478 – (Paperback)
ISBN – 9789948452485 – (E-Book)

Application Number: MC-10-01-8683051
Age Classification: E

Printer Name: iPrint Global Ltd
Printer Address: Witchford, England

First Published (2021)
AUSTIN MACAULEY PUBLISHERS FZE
Sharjah Publishing City
P.O Box [519201]
Sharjah, UAE
www.austinmacauley.ae
+971 655 95 202

This book is based on a proven best practice throughout a professional and remarkable HR track for more than 12 years.

Table of Contents

Introduction: The Model in Brief	13
HR Strategy Key Areas to Contemplate	16
HR Transition from Operational Focus to Strategic Focus Is No Longer an Option	*16*
HR-Organisation Strategy Alignment (The Ever-Long Struggle)	*19*
Organisation Culture and Its Role in Driving HR Strategy	*21*
Organisational Structure (Balancing the Soft and the Hard Sides of It)	*24*
Values and Ethics (The Soul of Your Strategy)	*30*
Recruitment	34
The Inevitable Recruitment Transformation	*34*
Recruitment Essentials	39
Workforce Requirements: Is It Numbers Only?	*40*
Searching for Talent	*47*
Competency-Based Selection	*50*
Onboarding	*57*
Recruitment and Technology	*65*
General Recruitment Policy Guidelines	*70*
The Four Levels Measurement: Introduction	72
Measuring Recruitment Effectiveness	*74*
Time to Hire	*75*
Cost Per Hire	*78*
New Hire Retention Percentage	*80*
100 − (Separations during probation period / Average headcount × 100)	*80*
Cost of Unfilled Vacancies	*80*

Recruitment Yield Ratios	*81*
Total Rewards	**86**
Introduction	*86*
Total Rewards Essentials	**91**
Total Rewards System Design	*91*
Compensation System Design	*93*
Job Evaluation	*94*
Point-Factor Method	*98*
Pay Structure Design	*106*
Compensation Systems	*109*
Compensation Systems Due Diligence	*111*
Measuring TR (Total Rewards) Effectiveness	*116*
Employment Brand: Introduction	**127**
Employment Brand Design	*130*
Employment Brand Execution	*135*
Employment Brand Evaluation	*136*
Training and Development	**138**
Introduction	*138*
Training and Development Essentials	**141**
Competency-Based Training	*141*
Leadership Competency-Based Development	*143*
HR-Led Learning Is a Success Factor	*148*
Creating A Culture of Learning	*150*
Selecting Training Programs	*153*
Measuring Training and Development Effectiveness	*155*
Training Hours Per Employee	*157*
Training Cost Per Employee	*158*
Training Cost to HR Cost	*158*
T&D ROI (Return On Investment)	*159*
Kirkpatrick's Model	*161*

Performance Management Essentials — 164
- *Creating a Culture of Star Performers* — 164
- *Performance Management System Framework* — 167
- *One to One: Performance Review* — 176
- *The Link Between Performance Management and Corporate Strategy* — 182
- *The Link Between Performance Management and TR* — 184
- *Competency-Based Performance Management* — 185
- *Performance Rating, Is It Obsolete?* — 186
- *Measuring Performance Management System Effectiveness* — 187

Performance Management System Scorecards — 193
- *Performance Management System – Internal Process.* — 193
- *Performance Management System – Employee Satisfaction.* — 193
- *Performance Management System – Learning and Growth.* — 193

Succession Management Essentials — 195
- *Talent Management* — 195
- *Succession Management Process* — 196
- *Measuring Succession Management Systems Effectiveness* — 198

Conclusion — 200

Introduction: The Model in Brief

It has all begun almost 12 years ago when I was exploring the world of human resources, I had the passion to discover the hidden areas of that field, to know more how what was called historically personnel managers turned to be strategic players advising and contributing to the C-suite level executives' strategies and goals.

At first, I was motivated by the new intricacies of my field, it was provoking my inner self on how to create a state that would set me apart from others. It was not easy at all, the expectations from the people surrounding me were very high, they were even a little bit unrealistic, everyone were hoping that the new HR guy equipped with the latest knowledge would far solve the inherent dilemmas in their departments. My short-sightedness at that time made me believe that I can solve those problems easily and effectively without referring to any kind of frameworks.

The first few years of my work in HR were mainly based on trial and error approach, I remember once when three new supervisors were promoted to a higher level, my manager asked me to prepare job descriptions for their new titles so they can be guided through their careers. The thing I did was to write few sentences that reflected the main aspects of the jobs without paying attention to the key elements of a proper job description (I will refer to them later during the book).

Another trait of my work was the inconsistency of my initiatives, I was delivering my plans on an ad hoc basis. This has resulted in a fragmented HR function, recruitment was carried out with no direct link to the company employment brand strategy, and total rewards were designed without linking them to the performance management system and the market rewards index and so on.

The outcome of such an approach was a fluctuated performance accompanied with fluctuated impact. This was not the impact I wanted nor was it satisfying my main goal, which is delivering a high-quality HR services with long lasting effect.

The turnaround point was exactly when I was attending a meeting about the strategic HR, it was an eye-opening experience at that time as I was searching on the best way to connect the fragmented HR functions I was pursuing. It took me several years after that meeting trying to connect the dots and conceptualising how can I establish an effective HR framework that could yield effective business results, the model as I visualise it is represented in Figure 1 (The Four

Levels of HR excellence). It's not all inclusive which means that there are many support functions and tools that you must have in place to supplement that model, I'll leave this to you to decide on as per your specific needs and demands. But the key elements of this model were vital for my success and to my company's overall HR effectiveness.

The model begins with what I call the Foundational HR Level (the first level) which consists of two major HR functions; the first one is the organisational brand and how to strengthen that brand through engagement and its impact on retention, the second one includes total rewards and recruitment as major parts of the HR service delivery strategy that formulate the corner stone of my HR department.

The second level (The Intermediate HR Level) includes two parts also, performance management and training and development. These two parts fall under the human capital development area that focuses mainly on the strategic part of this model.

The third level (Succession Management) is the crucial part of that model, in fact it has become a priority for all businesses all over the world. Executives, business owners and shareholders judge the effectiveness of the HR function according to the strength of its succession management strategies and how fast they can prepare successors in an ever-changing world. This level is the advance HR stage that builds on the previous two stages (the foundational and the intermediate), it's also an extension of the strategic part of the model.

At the top of that model comes the final stage which I call the Pinnacle which highlights the value of the whole model through the HR analytics. On the contrary to many prevalent HR analytics models I will talk about this vital part of the model in a concise way that will make it easy for you to absorb the details within this concept and thus giving you the leverage to apply immediately.

The previous stages in that model were selected as critical success factors for the success of my company at that time, there are many other HR functions that are important and should be in place to have a complete circle of the HR services required to maintain the employees' satisfaction and thus strengthening the EVP (Employee Value Proposition) e.g. the employees relations function is very important to maintain a healthy cooperative work environment and to avoid legal pitfalls in terms of labour agreements but usually it doesn't appear on the different HR frameworks implemented universally. Here I am not underestimating the function but rather I consider it one of the building blocks of an effective HR department but I would prefer to describe it as an embedded function within the overall HR arena.

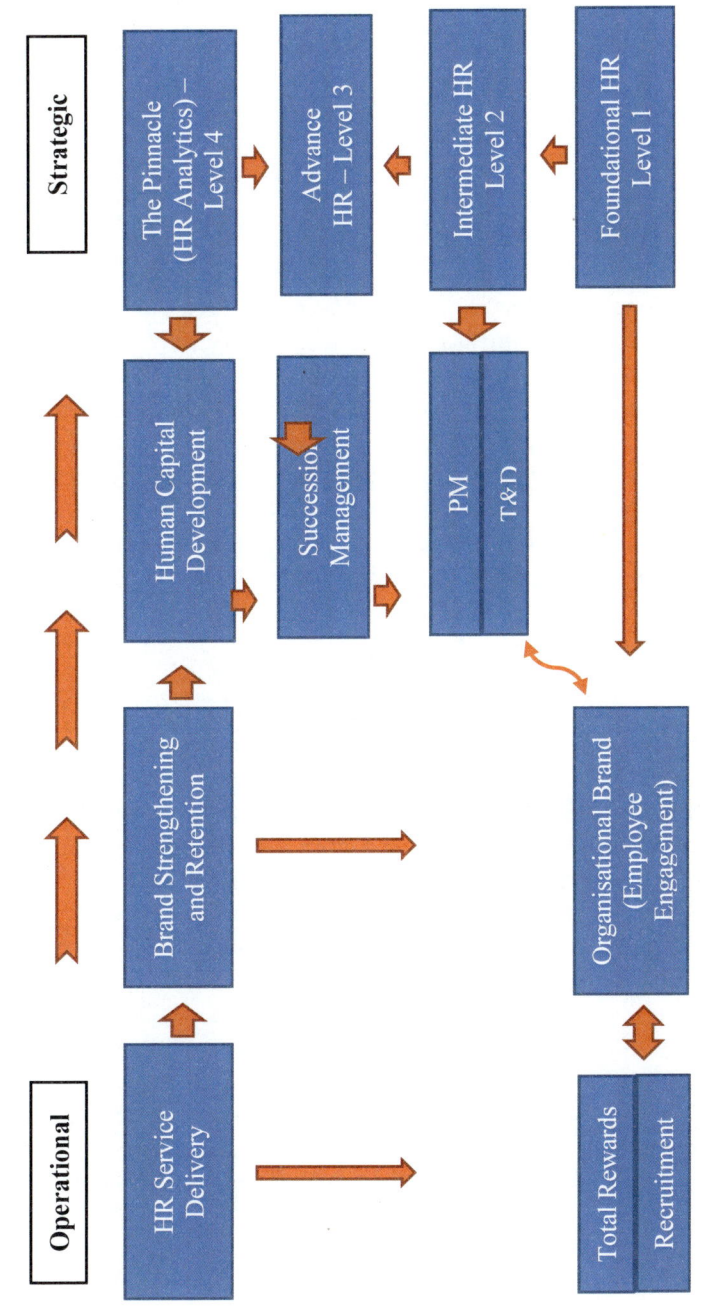

Figure 1 – The Four Levels of HR Excellence

HR Strategy Key Areas to Contemplate

HR Transition from Operational Focus to Strategic Focus Is No Longer an Option

Much has been said about the importance of shifting to a more strategic HR department but what has been done is not so much. I believe the HR profession was given a big momentum during the past few years to deliver the promised value to our stakeholders, we heard a lot of the buzzwords for HR as a business partner, the strategic player and many more concepts which were all putting more pressure on the function to deliver more.

Nothing is wrong in building the strategic capabilities of a function that was historically underestimated, but what was a big mistake is the absence of a robust assessment of the current reality of the people occupying the function. SHRM as the global leader of the HR services has introduced the HR competency study few years ago. Before that many years ago – roughly at the mid-90s – the HR profession was declared as a strategic function lying at the centre of the organisation.

All that momentum accompanied by the high level of expectations on the HR to deliver more with the absence of a clear roadmap on the needed guidance and direction for the people doing the real work has made our function fall short in a very dramatic way, I remember very well how many HR people whom I knew were forced to leave their companies because of not being able to achieve their business promises. Promises that I believe were unrealistic at that time.

What I propose here is to relook at our current capabilities (the HR folks) in terms of being able to master the HR basic functions and reshaping them in a way that support the broader business context, this will enable us to regain our lost credibility and on the other hand will lay out the foundation for a bigger role and active participation on a company-wide scale represented by offering the vital HR consultation for our stakeholders.

This journey that starts from putting the HR building blocks (the operational mode of HR) until reaching a higher senior role and status (the strategic mode of HR) within our organisations requires the following key steps to be acted upon and embraced:

1. Grasping the organisation's business and how it's being carried out throughout the different departments in the company; this important know-how is very vital to our presence and effectiveness in a very volatile work environment that no longer guarantees employment stability. Building this important competence which we call business acumen will not happen easily, we as HR professionals must strive in order to be aware of our business details, rarely that we can expect to go through a systematic cross-departmental orientation plan through which we can learn our business segments. You can notice that I mentioned the word orientation in the last sentence which emphasises that we don't need to be aware of every tiny detail in our business, rather we must build a general business knowledge that will make it easy for us to interact with the company managers in designing their people strategy without being afraid of not understanding the business terminologies. I recall clearly how I got my business acumen competency gradually through many ways. In some instances I asked people whom I trusted about a vague business concept that I didn't understand, in other cases I did my own research through the Internet and read comprehensively about certain topics through the company's literature; the result was a strong business acumen competency which contributed to my career growth in accelerated manner. Believe me, it's very effective and will save you many years and big effort to understand your business through a systematic way, but if your company's culture doesn't support that, don't wait for this to happen, go for it and get it in every possible way or else your career is doomed to fail and at the best case will be mediocre.
2. Acting in a proactive manner in offering HR consultation for our stakeholders. HR business partners behave differently than most of the tactical HR professionals, e.g. they don't wait for the sales manager to tell them that the revenue targets are not achievable because of sales workforce performance problems, rather they should step in and provide a solution in due time, this high response ability won't be easy if the HR person works in isolation and does not know what's happening around him or her. A key technique that I advise the HR people to follow is to ask stimulating questions during business meetings for any problem at hand, of course you need to take advantage when the opportunity comes and a manager introduces a pain in his/her department and is expecting an answer from you. Here you need to ask your questions in a way that would make the person reveal their concerns voluntarily. If you ask the sales manager why your salespeople haven't been successful in achieving their targets, you will get at most defensive answers with no real value for you to work on, while if you asked how can we find a better way to make your salespeople able to bring new revenue and/or customers for the company, most probably you will get insights that will help you to find the needed solution. Usually most of the HR persons rely on their HR systems (e.g. performance management system) to

design HR solutions according to their outcomes, but without paying attention to the highly dynamic nature of our businesses nowadays we are missing the golden opportunity to be a business architect that devise tailored solutions for business problems and on the spot, an advantage that we are compromising when we adopt a reactive mode in our work life.
3. Keeping pace with an ever fast changing profession. HR profession is one of the most evolving professions all over the world especially in the last twenty years, it was not so long time ago when we were reporting our achievements in activity-based approach, this level of reporting had detrimental effects on our profession in terms of describing the function as a pure qualitative discipline that lacks a rigorous quantitative approach that would put it on the front line of the business. Now we are talking about HR analytics as a make or break element in our HR business models, this is a key aspect within the accelerated development loop of the HR profession that we must master as quickly as possible or else we will be behind the curve, there are many other more important updates in the HR more than we can imagine and yet the most surprising updates are to come! Someone could ask, how being updated with the recent changes in the HR field could make me a strategic partner. The answer is so easy, being a strategic partner requires that you give consultation to your senior management when required to do so, a consultant's key strength and competence is their knowledge and we hear a lot about many management consultants all over the world and the level of the big effort they exert to be updated with their fields of specialty. The same thing applies for us as HR professionals, being updated with the latest changes in our field will give us the capacity to be effective consultants to our companies.

There are many other areas to cover as HR professionals in order to move our ship into the right direction so we can reach the strategic level that will differentiate us from others and will give us the pass card to the C-level gate. I will mention here the ability to prepare effective leadership organisational capability as an example. The above mentioned three points were very influential in my career progression, you can gain insights from them to develop your strategic competence but it's very important to design your own development path, a path that reflects your current reality and what works best for you.

Ignoring today's reality of the advance maturity level that HR has reached will put us behind the curve and will definitely prevent us from transitioning to the strategic side of HR, so it's not really a wise option to stay at the operational side of HR. It's the time to leap to a new stage of our careers, a stage that must be easily described by others as strategic in its nature and deliberate by its evolution.

HR-Organisation Strategy Alignment (The Ever-Long Struggle)

It has been a big dilemma – the issue of HR strategy alignment with the main company goals and strategies. The big disconnect between HR and the senior management and the lack of their involvement in the strategy decision making and execution has even widened the gap.

Historically HR has been an admin function that supported the employees' daily needs in terms of compensation plans execution, health benefits plans administration…etc. The slow progress of the function for the decades before the 90s has framed the function in a reactive mode for many years; this has deprived us from priceless learning experiences that other functions like sales and finance have gone through and become very much matured when it comes to participating effectively in business conversations and offering business solutions that are up to the management satisfaction.

The time is still in our favour, although the development pace of our function has been faster than we can afford in some cases, especially in the last ten years it had its positive effect on us. SHRM as I stated earlier has introduced the SHRM competency model, a model that was derived from a universal research that captured the opinions of many HR stakeholders on the critical success factors for our excellence in HR, many competencies ranging from business acumen to global and cultural effectiveness accompanied by valid assessment tools to help gauge our proficiency level in these competencies and others have been the corner stone in our career development journey.

This is just a one key example on the big array of HR tools, programs and many other ways that we can use to develop our careers. Now that we are equipped with the needed support structure that can boost our development in a fast track way, we can catch up the queue.

After we have achieved the needed level of our career proficiency then we can move forward to aid in the organisational strategy formulation by adding up the people section to the main strategy. But it's not just a matter of crafting a well-designed HR strategy that contains the best practices that aims to have a prestigious HR department; indeed, it should be a subsequent goal after strengthening the organisation's HR capabilities. We strengthen this capability by aligning our actions, goals and ultimately our HR business strategies to the organisational top-level strategies.

How can we achieve that alignment? The word alignment means an arrangement in which two or more things (In this context they are the HR and the organisation strategies) are put together to achieve harmony. Clear and simple concept to understand but very difficult to apply in reality.

Alignment is not a one-time event that happens at certain point of your strategic planning process or action plans execution. It should be continuous and responsive effort when needed and as required. Usually any planning for any department lies under three main categories; Strategy Design, Strategy Execution and Strategy Evaluation. Each of these stages has its own alignment reaction mode as illustrated in Figure 2.

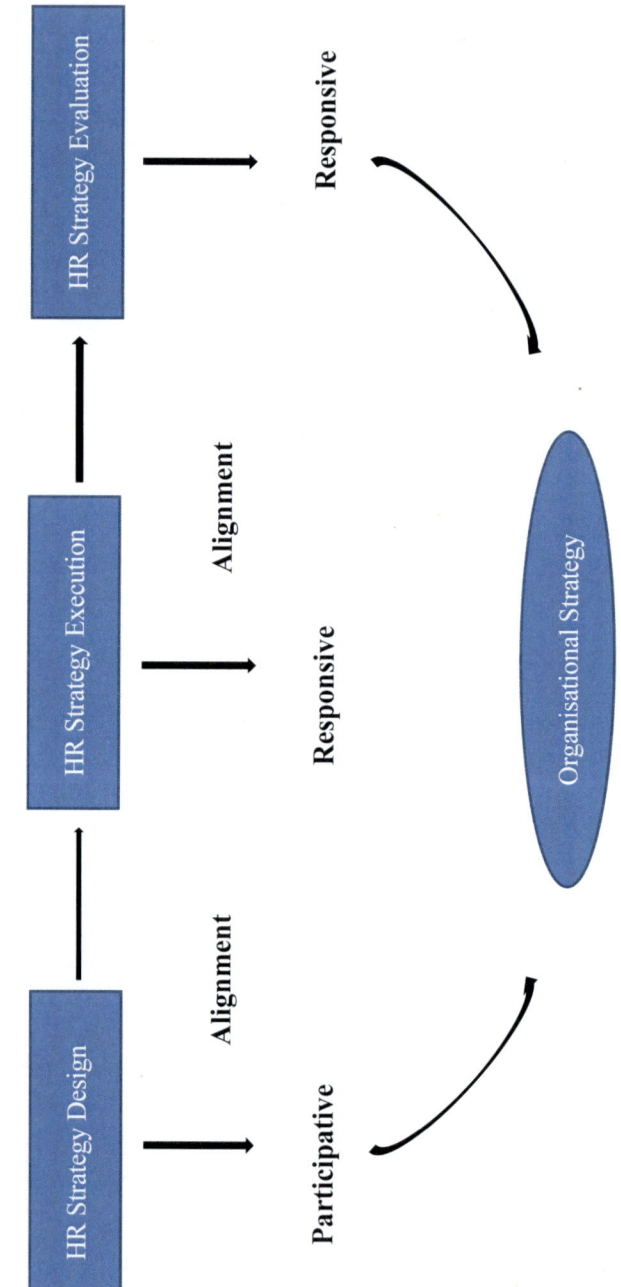

Figure 2 – HR-Organisation Strategy Alignment

The first stage (HR Strategy Design) is based on a participative alignment effort if we supposed that HR is already a mature function within the organisation that has its place on the table. Through this stage HR tries to understand the organisation HR needs and how to satisfy them, an example of this stage would be hiring new production personnel in order to achieve the organisation goals of increasing the production lines outputs, HR effort at this stage is easy.

In the second stage (HR Strategy Execution) HR alignment effort is responsive; it means that HR responds to the changes that happen to the organisation's strategy governed by changes in the internal or external environment and adjust its strategy. Acting in a proactive manner as I mentioned in point number two in the previous topic would be a vital thing to guarantee that changes in HR strategy are timely and effective. As an example of this stage HR would suggest hiring production workers with advance technology skills as the new production lines technology requires such calibre. If HR didn't respond when needed to support the organisation strategy it means that either HR is being highly involved at the design stage and excluded at the execution stage or it could mean that HR is highly involved in both the design and the execution stages but is not so effective in predicting changes and reacting to them properly.

The final stage (HR Strategy Evaluation) is characterised also by a responsive effort but these efforts to adjust HR strategy in most cases are of low value. HR at this stage suggest changes to its strategies after completing the cycle of the organisation strategy which means that if any harm has happened at the organisational level then HR reaction to adjust strategy for the next period won't make a big deference. If HR has listed in its strategy for the next cycle the training of the new production workers to accommodate the technology advancement in the production lines then this would mean unnecessary high cost that could have been avoided if HR had acted effectively at the first and the second stage.

If you follow through these three stages with alertness in your ability to act on every stage you will guarantee that your alignment effort is effective and your overall human capital strategy is serving the ultimate goals of the organisation.

Organisation Culture and Its Role in Driving HR Strategy

In this section I will not go into the details of the organisational culture contradictions and how to take advantage of them to help support the HR strategy implementation. This is not to undermine this aspect of the cultural variations and their effect on any company rather I will focus on how to take advantage of the organisational cultural strength and common traits to support the strategy implementation.

Before we begin this section, I want to define the culture from my own perspective and how I see it through many years of working with many people; it's the beliefs, values and principles that guide employees' behaviours, yes, it is, but still is not reflecting my own personal perspective. It's the way how we do our work on daily basis, yes, it is, but still I need to have it more customised to reflect my own personal perspective. **It's the repetitive routines and**

behaviours that happen continuously and deliberately forming the organisation's collective identity that it becomes nearly impossible to change its components.

Usually most of the HR function effort to study the organisational culture begins from the premise that we need to know. First, what are the cultural components of our employees and the differences that lie between them then neutralising the undesirable aspects of the culture and focusing more on the desirable aspects of the culture to our benefit.

It's true, but it could take you several years to understand the cultural components of any organisation and you will never reach a complete understanding of your culture, e.g. in some cases you are sure that your employees' communication style is mostly indirect which you build on most of your communication plans. This means that you could highlight on the key areas only of your HR strategy communication in a presentation you are making to your line managers, taking into consideration that the details are not so important for people whom you worked with for many years and who trust you well, but to find in the middle of your presentation that one manager challenges you to justify the importance of the new onboarding to her department. The reason for that could be that you mentioned that this program's main target is to reduce the turnover rate for the new comers within their first year of employment and the manager who challenged you perceived that this program is geared toward her because her department had the highest turnover rate for the last year although you didn't mean that.

What I want to emphasise here that you can't predict the human behaviour as it's so complex and trying to quantify this complexity will literally put you in a maze. Why waste our time trying to navigate through the details of the culture and in turn excluding others who don't match the common traits and values of your organisation while you can search for the simple core traits that everyone can accept that will form your super power to help achieve any plan you have in place.

I remember clearly how I tried for many years to enforce my HR plans without paying attention to the cultural identity of my company, it has led me over and over to a definite failure, but when I started looking at that overlooked aspect of the organisation's DNA, the overall performance and achievement rate of my department went up. In my company the majority of the line managers wanted and accepted the HR agenda I was introducing in many cases as long as they didn't bear the responsibility of the execution and in turn won't be held accountable on the end results (which I believe to be a common theme in too many workplaces).

It was a turning point for me to accept that truth at that time and trying to fix it by holding myself a shared responsibility of the outcomes, it was not the right thing to do because after many years I became a very big proponent that the HR department is the only department within any organisation that designs its plans and implement them for the benefit of the other departments while the rest of the departments design and implement their plans for their own benefits.

My success was limited because taking the charge of my plans that way will lead at best to a short-term effect, the right approach is usually represented by holding my managers responsible and holding them accountable for the results. Building on that knowledge I started working on my plans years after that by directing the responsibility to its right place (the line managers). I expected that would solve the problem as it's the right action to do to guarantee my success, but still the results were not as required.

I am pretty sure that applying the conventional wisdom in this situation was not the right intervention to embrace, so how did I solve the problem? I decided that this time I will leave it to them (the line managers) to decide on the most suitable approach for them to absorb my plans. By this I mean not only the implementation approach but even it could be to adjust the way in how the plan was designed.

Performance management system was a real example of this cultural dilemma, this system has been in place for few years and the effort that I exerted to implement the system was so great but the yield was so little, I was trying to apply my own agenda without paying attention to the line managers' agendas. The big burden of the performance management system and its related forms and the steps it has taken to be completed was so overwhelming to the degree that all my effort over three years was irrelevant and the system was not completely successful.

When I involved the managers in the system implementation for the first time the results were represented in a better understanding of the system's purpose and its benefits, although the way they adopted to implement the system was unique (they suggested to shift to a two-way conversation based system that focuses on coaching and achieving results) and a little bit risky in terms of its success rate the expected results were very optimistic and promising. We expect the system to be rolled out successfully this time as the managers are the ones who crafted the system's new changes although 'till that moment the expected benefits of the new system have not materialised yet.

In this case I focused on a simple one core element in our culture, it's the Authorization I gave to my line managers to apply the system the way they like it to be implemented. Although the word authorisation is paralleled with permission which could be misunderstood, it was a key forming element of our culture and trying to change that element would be like trying to move a mountain from its place, the right thing to do is to climb the mountain carefully in order not to fall while climbing and pass it on to another one.

After many years I realised that working through the culture is the safest approach to thrive in your work and in turn succeeding in any plan you might have. Try to break the culture and it will break you apart, work through the culture and it will work for you!

Organisational Structure (Balancing the Soft and the Hard Sides of It)

Many years ago, I had a talk with an HR colleague about an HR consultation project that he undertook, he was bragging that he has accomplished a lot during that project. He talked about preparing comprehensive job descriptions for every single title in the company, also he talked about the HR policies and procedures manual he had accomplished in addition to many other HR aspects, most importantly he focused on the organisational structure he had designed for the company. 'It's all great what you have done,' I said to him after he finished his talk and asked him a question. 'Do you believe that drawing some boxes that are connected with reporting lines will solve the structural challenges for that organisation?'

He paused for a moment with his facial expression confirming his loss and his inability to respond, then he said, 'I've done my part of the deal and designed for them a flat organisational structure that should help support their goals.' I didn't say anything after his comment, not because I didn't want to embarrass him with my answer but because I didn't know what the answer was.

Years after that and after going through many experiences I realised that the most important thing when it comes to organisational structure is the awareness level the employees in the company have about the organisation structure and the main roles for every function within this structure and how they interrelate with each other. This issue is very easy to execute, all what you need is just to have your organisational structure published on your bulletin board and to have your doors (of HR department) open to others so they can come to you whenever they have a question about this organisational structure.

The important question here is how we can get to that level of awareness; the answer is straightforward and goes into a sequence of three stages:

1. **The First Stage:** at this level HR must continuously update the organisational structure either through the updates that happen through the work flow changes (promotions, demotions, transfers...etc.) or through knowing the updates that will happen on the organisational level through business meetings and their effects on the organisation and reflecting them appropriately on the org. chart. This is the basic level of the structural changes and it's only about having accurate and consistent documentation that reflects up to date org. structure.
2. **The Second Stage:** at this level HR must step in and to provide the best advice on the best org. structure that fits the current situation of the organisation. I will not go into the details of the structural arrangements and how to design a proper structure (e.g. advising the executive management to shift to a product-based structure for product X that has its dedicated resources and functions to operate more freely in order to respond effectively to the competition in the marketplace). This knowledge is very important and vital for us as HR professionals, it will add on our knowledge reservoir and will increase our credibility as

business partners. You need to master that piece of your technical HR expertise but within this context I will focus again on our role as trusted advisors to our line managers. Our main role is to monitor the work activities of the various departments (tapping into your business acumen competency) and to sense when there are bottlenecks that hinder a smooth work flow. Usually a natural response in such cases is to bring new people onboard as a reaction to this state which appears as a more workload or lack of organising skills. Those areas could be a reason for the bottlenecks but what most of us don't pay attention to is how the employees within each function are mapped under the right jobs. You could have the best HR structure that has a dedicated HR specialist for every function (the rationale behind this is to provide a value-added service through experts who design tailored HR solutions for the business problems) but to find that this solution didn't pay dividends, in this case one of the recruitment specialists didn't have the required candidate relationship management skill that will lead to more new hires yield ratio. The other factors like having state-of-the-art ATS (Applicant Tracking System) or the skills needed to do behavioural interview won't be of a much value if the preceding element (candidate relationship management) is not there. I conclude this discussion by saying that advising the management about the best structure includes many aspects but a key factor to have a successful structure is to match the right person to the most suitable job or function supposed that the other support elements (the tools, resources and the right structural arrangement) are available.

3. **The Third Stage:** we talked in the first two stages about the continuous update that HR must maintain for the org. structure and how to have the best structure through having the best people occupying the most suitable job. Now and in order to complete the chain we need to provide the HR structure that would serve the major org. structure and ultimately making the needed alignment. Through HR structures you have many options; you could rely on a dedicated or functional HR structure or you can choose to have a shared services structure with the full spectrum or to choose some elements from it as per your business needs. Again, I will not talk about the details of those alternatives because HR literature contains a lot of information about them. I will talk here about two main issues, the first one is how to select a proper HR structure that evolves organically and the second one is how to maintain a nimble HR structure that changes according to the organisational circumstances. All the departmental structures evolve in response to the organisational life cycle stage and HR is no exception to that rule. At the beginning of the life cycle of the organisation (Start-up) HR is a generalist function that undertakes all the HR duties, although at certain point of this stage HR generalists would face the problem of balancing the priorities of the big load of their duties (e.g. deciding whether to execute the urgent hiring of

three production workers that requires screening tens of resumes manually and their related complementary procedures or the pressing demands of finalising the paper-based performance management system). This stage is really beneficial to the development path of any HR professional, I personally went through this experience! It taught me how to organise and manage my tasks effectively, most importantly it gave me the privilege of building my different HR experiences first-hand which I built upon the rest of my advance HR career. At later stages of the organisational life cycle HR begins to formulate a specialised identity mainly for all the HR functions. At the early growth stage you can see for example that HR has more than the one person HR department, there are many HR generalists but usually they do the same work, this stage is a little bit risky for HR because if no clear boundaries are set between those HR generalists, an overlap is inventible and in turn will lead to work redundancy and if not managed well the chaos is the prevalent trait. At the third stage (The Complete Growth Stage) the burden of the HR tasks is unbearable and a big delay in the work execution is common trait of the function in addition to acute mistakes that could happen, the work flow is totally paralysed. At this stage it becomes vital for the HR function to begin the specialisation journey, you begin to separate the HR's various functions into individual units and to create HR specialists who represent the recruitment, training and development, performance management functions and many other HR domains. By embracing this approach, you can mitigate the risk of totally losing control of your HR department, but a negative effect has already happened. Here comes the positive effect of having an organically developed HR structure, not a structure that transforms itself reactively when the changes happen. Seasoned HR professionals can anticipate the upcoming business events and/or expansions and in turn taking the needed action immediately. Having an organic developed HR structure is merely about having skilled and forward-looking HR professionals who can make the structural changes in the right time so they can prepare for the new structure properly. (Transitioning form a functional to dedicated HR structure requires a different set of skills and expertise). It's a skill that they can harness by developing the business acumen competency which gives them an advantage of leaping ahead of time and adjusting their structure as it serves the business needs so once the change happens the right structure is already in place and functioning well. At the maturity stage the organisation reaches the highest level of growth rate in its market, HR could respond either by increasing the number of the HR specialists or it could adapt a totally new structure like the shared services. At the Decline Stage (the final stage) HR begins to retract, at best HR structure remains as is with the possibility of decreasing the number of HR people within the structure. In this case the company is able to keep a certain level of income and profits that maintains its existence. If the financial situation of the organisation goes bad then the decline will affect the HR structure drastically and a big change like eliminating some functions or merging two functions together could happen. In Figure 3 I depict the organisation life cycle and its impact on the HR structure. The impact on HR as represented in this figure is only an example which means that this impact could be represented in different HR structures and functions. This impact on HR differs according to many factors e.g. the organisation activities, the industry, the strategic agility of the HR department and how and when they respond…etc.

Figure 3 – Organisational Life Cycle Impact on HR Structure

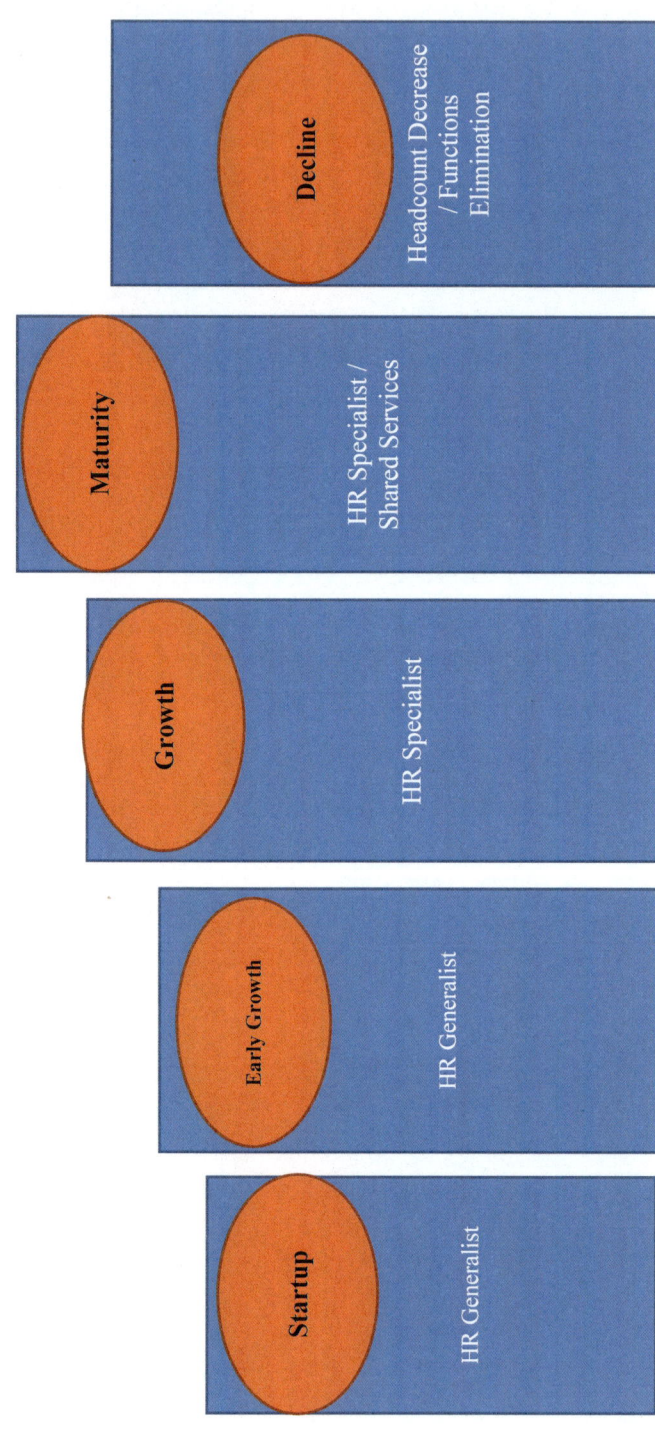

The aforementioned three stages in one way or another represent the hard side of the structural arrangements of the HR department. It's the discipline that study the organisational needs and to design the best structure possible that serve those needs from an HR perspective.

Now we will talk about the soft side of the organisational structure. Suggesting the best HR structure doesn't necessarily mean that the organisation's work flow will not be interrupted; here I am answering our friend who consulted one organisation on a flat structure that he expected will solve the problems of that organisation, what's the benefit if you have a flat structure but the culture of the organisation doesn't support neither maintains the structure. We defined the culture at the beginning of this book as the repetitive behaviours that happen continuously, so if the managers in the organisation are used to autocratic management style (which naturally creates a tall organisational structure) then forcing a flat structure would definitely lead to inconsistency between the announced structure and its execution.

When it comes to this important side of our work the first thing we need to tackle are the behaviours of the managers occupying the structure, of course, changing behaviours to adapt to the most suitable structure for the business strategy won't happen overnight, you need to educate your management about the importance of behaviour adaptability as the key to the success in your organisation in all the aspects including an effective nimble organisational structure. Failing to adjust your behaviours as necessitated by your work environment and its consequences will force your business to be adjusted to the environment coercively. In our last example failing to execute the flat structure because of the change resistance from the managers will make the transformation to self-directed teams nearly impossible, this won't make a difference when the organisation is at early stages of the global expansion but once it reaches the global maturity the slow pace of behaviour change is absolutely disastrous to the organisation and could lead to the demise of the organisation, at least to the level of outside the headquarter borders.

In order to make sure your efforts are successful changing behaviours should be gradual to a degree that doesn't interfere with the organisation's progress. This means that if the slowly changing behaviours are blocking your organisation's success, you need to make fast and drastic changes even to your current management team in order to survive in a fast-paced world. In an ideal case where the time factor is in our favour, we need to take advantage of that rare opportunity and begin to prepare the managers for a new set of behaviours that should support our current structure.

In this context I will give you a small advice, make some minor changes to the way your managers are dealing with their employees so it would serve your goal without causing any defects from the sudden change shock that most of us get trapped in. In a hierarchical culture it would be a wise thing to do by asking your managers to give their employees some latitude in the decision-making process and making the final decision authority under their control so they won't feel completely powerless. In such case a production manager gives the supervisors below her the empowerment to study the cost effectiveness of adjusting the production machines as per the new standards as requested by customers through the customer satisfaction survey. The manager reviews the major outcomes of the study and adjust some minor issues and then approves the decision. In a different scenario where the production manager interfered with all the details this would have caused a delay in the machine's new standards adjustment and thus affecting badly the customer loyalty in addition to the bad level of the morale for the current supervisors who didn't have the opportunity to learn new experiences and thus limiting their career progression.

Another important factor that we must take into consideration to make the cultural transformation needed to apply the new organisational structure is the trust level between the managers and their employees. Any kind of initiative, process enhancement, new procedures implementation…etc. requires a high trust level between the stakeholders of that initiative. You can't deploy successfully the new engagement measurement tool in your company if the trust between employees and management is weak (maybe due to similar past bad experience). In this context trust plays an important role but not as much as the role it plays in deploying a new org. structure. Referring back to our last example if the manager improved the trust with his subordinates before the engagement survey cycle then we can expect to some degree that the employees will reveal some of their concerns when filling out the survey, but when it comes to a big initiative like the new org. structure execution, trust must be maintained consistently because the issue of the org. structure is not a onetime event that happens every once in a while, it's a lifetime practice that affects every single area you can imagine in the organisation so varying trust levels will lead definitely to a fragmented structure. Trust is the cure to any resistance in your company. Employees will do anything for their managers if they believe in heart that the trust between them is mutual.

Bottom line is, the success of any organisational structure depends on having both the hard side (the structure design) and the soft side of the structure (the culture that supports the structure execution) functioning smoothly and in parallel.

Values and Ethics (The Soul of Your Strategy)

It's well-known that most of the organisational strategies and plans begin with this area as the first thing to tackle before anything else. Although true, I delayed the discussion about it till now for one main reason; values and ethics are the first things we begin with when preparing HR plans but it's the last thing we remember when we move forward to the tangible areas of HR. In this context I don't mean that you need to tackle this issue lastly because it's the foundation from which every single aspect of the other organisational design elements build upon. Here I am reinforcing the importance of reviewing these values again once we finish making the organisational plans. The purpose of this review is to notice any deviation from the core values that we embedded when we began our strategic planning efforts.

Usually and as applicable in most organisations the values cascade stems out from both the vision and mission statements of the organisation; at that level the executive management sets the tone for the rest of the organisation for the behaviours that should guide the mission execution. Here I will emphasise again on the importance of the alignment between the organisational goals and the values that are spelled out by the management. Most of the executive people whom I worked with didn't achieve the needed level of the compatibility between the organisational strategies and its values. They either say something that is aligned with their goals but is not supported through their performance management system and their culture in a broader sense (e.g. specifying customer excellence as one of the values but actually the after sales service personnel don't have the performance standards that guide their behaviour) or most dangerously they act on values that are disconnected from their strategy framework (e.g. identifying the geographic expansion as a key target in order to increase sales revenue from Product A but the current sales team is focusing on irrelevant behaviours that support tactical goals like increasing the delivery time to customers).

In the two cases the results are mediocre although in the second one (the disconnected values from the main strategies) the path to recover is too long. In this case you need first to identify a set of core values that match your strategies then you need to guarantee that these values are embraced in a day-to-day basis.

In order to create a value-based workplace and to make sure that our values are serving our purpose and are aligned with our organisational goals, executives must go through the following sequence in order to identify the core values for their organisations:

1. The first step in this endeavour is to assess the current culture, to know the prevalent behaviours that affect the way how the employees are interacting with each other. There are multiple ways to do that; it could be through observation from an experienced superior who is familiar with the working environment and in turn identifying the critical behaviours for the success of the organisation, practically it is rare to apply such a solution because it is difficult to find a neutral person who can make this assignment. A better approach is to have a systematic way to identify the current behaviours through for example conducting focus groups that represent all the departments in the organisation.
2. After identifying the critical behaviours (values) the following model must be followed:

- The managers in the organisation must reinforce a compliant workplace by making the values and the critical behaviours very clear through repeating those norms in many communication ways like meetings, coaching…etc. (e.g. Integrity is an important value that the sales manager should make it clear for his sales team, that doing business with prospected customers must be based solely on selling the product value

and not trying unethical ways like offering pay-outs to decision makers in the target company).
- Ensuring the Fairness in any practices that affect the employees and their work. If the managers in any organisation are dealing fairly with the employees the trust can be built but if unfair practices are prevalent in the workplace, distrust will be seen obviously and it will affect the performance.
- Mangers must motivate their employees based on modelling the critical behaviours (Values) because the employees are always monitoring their managers and whether they are applying fair practices or not.
- Through following the previous three steps the potential that the employees will make the critical behaviours part of their work life will increase and in turn laying the foundation for a value-based workplace culture.

3. The final step is to maintain the desired values; they will be maintained through the role modelling from the leaders as mentioned above, but as a best practice it is preferred to integrate the critical behaviours for the organisation within the leadership competency framework. In other words the leadership development won't be based only on a job-based qualification, rather it should include the critical behaviours as a key component of the leadership development process. The person must show an ethical behaviour in his/her leadership practices to be nominated for a future leadership role.

Let's suppose that we reached the level where the values are of match to the organisational strategies and goals in terms of their compatibility and execution, how can we guarantee that these values will serve as the key driver of the company success?

Following solely through the previous model (Achieving a Value-Based Workplace) won't bring any organisation the optimal workplace with its full behavioural capacity to make any kind of transformation. Keeping the organisational atmosphere functioning at the highest level possible requires for organisational leaders as I said before to be role models and most importantly for them to hold themselves accountable before anyone else if/when they deviate from their assigned course of action. It's well-known that one of our shortcomings as human beings is our internal bias to our preconceived ideas which will make a block to move ourselves to a new state and thus accepting the new behaviours as our new way of life. The other important shortcoming is our resistance to accept criticism from others, so how would it be easy to criticise ourselves. So, the key question here, how can we beat these shortcomings? We have two ways, the first one is reinventing ourselves every once in a while, by making a rigorous self-review for our mistakes and any behaviour deviation from the core values of the organisation. This approach should come as a natural response to this behavioural dilemma but it requires that the leaders have a high degree of discipline to make that change. In today's business world rarely we can find leaders who have this ability so it's more rational and effective to go through the second option. According to this approach leaders use a deliberate approach to fix this dilemma. One of the effective ways is to use self-profiles that uncover the hidden personality traits of the person. It helps leaders to navigate through their psychology which will give them the needed knowledge on their shortcomings without going through the traditional way of the trial and error approach (to do mistakes and to learn from them) and most probably most of us won't notice any self-deficiency because of the self-bias we all have. There are many available online tools that we can use to reach this level of self-awareness but the most important thing to do before we go through this experience is to prepare ourselves for the shock after doing the profile. As I mentioned before that most of us have fears of facing the reality of our weakness and in most cases such fear is destructive to the process of self-discovery and the action plan to adjust the behaviour as needed.

It's okay when going through the stage of self-discovery to feel uncomfortable of facing yourself or even sometimes to feel angry. Using these emotions of anger as positive momentum to steer our development can be beneficial to make the behaviour change otherwise to surrender to these emotions will definitely cause a big harm and will prevent us from progressing. I didn't describe these emotions as negative because emotions whether we see them as negative or positive are merely emotions and we can use them both to our benefit or detriment, e.g. not sharing your happiness in gaining a budget approval on HR initiative with your team instantly won't serve as a leverage to the current level of employees morale.

Once we pass our fears we can now move to the next step which is putting the action plan for our self-development. The action plan should target the behaviours that are essential to our development (e.g. it's important for you as an HR manger to adjust your confrontational style of conflict resolution to more a collaborative approach when needed rather than focusing on adjusting your analytical-based decision-making tendency). In this example it's important to take into consideration other factors in your decision making other than facts and figures but it's more important to focus on building different conflict resolution styles and behaviours in a career stage where you are being exposed to a broader scope of the organisational stakeholders. Actually, the change rhythm when it comes to adjusting behaviour will be slow, but by relying on valid tools to discover ourselves the journey to achieve our goal would be much easier.

After identifying the action plan to improve our shortcomings the second important thing is to monitor the workplace in order to keep it aligned with the core values of the company. Here I will reinforce the role of the line managers in keeping the current culture aligned with the desired values. This rank (the middle management) is the link between the upper management and the rest of the company and by focusing our efforts on enabling this group to disseminate a value-based workplace we will guarantee that our values will be lived in action.

Recruitment

The Inevitable Recruitment Transformation

As depicted in Figure 1 the recruitment function is considered one of the foundational blocks for any successful HR department (it was located under the HR service delivery arena). HR service delivery concept could reach every single aspect in the HR department so the functions lying under it are not inclusive. Here I am reinforcing again that the model in Figure 1 reflects my own perspective in managing the HR department I worked in for the last 12 years.

In brief, HR service delivery concept is about designing your HR strategies, goals and programs while keeping eye on serving your stakeholders and dealing with them as if they were your customers. Under this concept you offer the best service possible to your stakeholders according to their needs and what they see is relevant to their plans and goals by designing customised HR programs that fit their departments. It's a revolution on the old method of designing HR discreet programs that looks to the organisation from the HR angle only. In our topic it was dominant decades ago that the HR function helped the organisational departments in the recruitment activities in a traditional way, the focus was on providing the needed number of employees only without focusing on organisation-individual cultural match for example which is considered a key element of a successful recruitment strategy in addition to many other important elements that guarantee an effective recruitment function.

In our highly competitive world, the success of any organisation depends first and foremost on the people whom the company is employing, it doesn't matter if you have the best strategy making team or the best technology and your employees are not up to your expectations. Many studies have proved that the companies that select their employees carefully achieves more productivity and efficiency than the companies that do the recruitment in a traditional way. Also the successful companies focus a lot during their recruitment process on delivering their message of what it's like to work in the company and what does it expect from these candidates to deliver on their jobs to serve the mission of the organisation. Such practices are of utmost importance and are considered a competitive edge that can contribute to achieve the organisational goals.

Recruitment function has evolved a lot during the past few years, recruiters are no longer the operational guys who are doing their jobs according to what they get from the people above them; they have become a real marketer who promote for their company's employment and through the process they deal with the employment candidates as if they were there valuable customers. But before going through this concept let's go back to define the recruitment as we all know it and to highlight also on the recruitment stages.

Recruitment is the process that aims to attract the candidates outside the organisation to apply for the vacant jobs into the organisation. It goes through the following four stages **(Taken from SHRM Foundation's Effective Practice Guidelines Series – Recruiting and Attracting Talent.** James A. Breaugh, Ph.D. Recruiting and Attracting Talent, A Guide to Understanding and Managing Recruitment Process. SHRM Foundation, 2009**.):**

1. **Establishing Recruitment Objectives:** during this stage you should identify the following:

   - Number of open positions to be filled.
   - Date by which positions should be filled.
   - Number of applications desired.
   - Type of applicants sought:
     - Level of education.
     - Knowledge, skills and abilities.
     - Interests and values.
   - Job performance goals for new hires.
   - Expected new-hire retention rate.

2. **Develop Recruitment Strategy:** The purpose of developing a recruitment strategy is to establish a specific plan of attaining recruitment objectives through asking the following questions:

   - What type of individuals should be targeted?
   - Where can these people be found?
   - How can the targeted individuals best be reached?
   - What recruitment message should be communicated?
   - What type of recruiters should be used?
   - What should a job offer entail?

To guarantee the effectiveness in addressing the previous questions we need to segment the recruitment cycle into separate phases and to see how prospective job candidates view the whole process through the following questions:

   - How well does the person feel the organisation is interested in him or her?
   - Does the recruitment message directly address why a person should apply?
   - Is the recruitment message believable?

3. **Carry Out Recruitment Activities:** the next step is to carry out the recruitment activities such as advertising on job boards or hosting

receptions on university campuses. HR should take into consideration the results of selected activities through conducting proper recruitment metrics.
4. **Measurement and Evaluation of Recruitment Results:** When evaluating recruiting process, we need to look for two major things:

- Gathering information on recruitment outcomes through the following metrics.
  * Time-to-hire.
  * Cost of filling the position.
  * New employee retention date.
  * New employee performance level.
  * Hiring manager's satisfaction with the recruitment process.
  * Applicants' perceptions of the recruitment process.

- Demonstrate to HODs what is the value for the organisation from this process.
  * Some of the factors to be taken into consideration when gathering data on the efficiency of the recruitment process.
    - Number of the new hires yielded from the recruitment sources.
    - New hires who receive the strongest performance review during the first year.
    - Number of new hires who stayed for the organisation the longest.
    - Contact applicants who are aware of the opening but didn't apply.

I mentioned before the concept of the traditional recruitment and the progress that we witnessed in the recruitment until we reached the current status of what we call the recruitment marketing. In order to understand the modern concept of recruitment marketing we must make a comparison between recruitment and marketing.

Marketing is the function through which the company provides and/or introduces a value to its customers through its products and/or services for the purpose of building solid relationships with these customers which in turn will create a value for the company (The value here represents the revenue and the loyalty to the company brand).

Let's now define the recruitment from a marketing perspective. Within this context recruitment is the function through which the company provides a value to the company's candidates through building a unique candidate experience through the recruitment stages and thus creating a value to the company (The value here is represented by a successful conversion for the candidates into permanent employees and by strengthening the employment brand in addition to the big pool of candidates that the company will build). An example of creating value to the candidates would be in providing RJP (Realistic Job Preview) of the company and the nature of its work even if it was a difficult one like the jobs that involve working in remote areas with harsh environment conditions.

There is a similarity between the two concepts, and I will break it down into the following two points:

1. Both functions' (Marketing and Recruitment Marketing) main goal is to provide value to their customers.
2. Both functions provide value in favour of receiving value.

So, the common word between the two functions is the Value, and the value creation when it comes to recruitment has multiple options; these options revolve around what we call the touch points (another marketing concept). Recruitment touch points are the occasions where the company interacts with its candidates, it usually has a resulting outcome that is either positive or negative and it affects to a great extent the candidates' judgement on whether to join the company or not. Touch points are illustrated in Figure 4.

Figure 4 – Recruitment Touchpoints

The rationale behind this concept is to build a positive candidate experience which ultimately will strengthen the employer brand (I will talk about it in more detail in the subsequent sections).

Building a positive candidate experience is not a one-time event, as illustrated above it goes into a cyclic approach that must repeat itself over and over. At the same time the stages in the recruitment touchpoints model are interrelated. If the hiring managers in your company were biased to certain qualities and they discarded qualified people who don't have these qualities then you can't expect these candidates to have a total positive experience just because they were amazed when they met you in the elegant booth you had in your town job fair.

It doesn't also serve you to be fair at your testing procedure and you don't have a proper onboarding system in place.

Professional recruiters who adopt the recruitment marketing methodology tend to examine the factors in the above model (these factors are not inclusive) continuously while asking the following questions:

- What are the most important factors that the candidates really valued?
- What are the factors that they didn't like?
- What factors that should be strengthened and maintained and what factors that should be improved or eliminated?

The answers to these questions will constitute a blueprint that will guide you through your candidate experience journey.

Historically recruitment has been underestimated mainly because of the slowness of that function in providing the qualified employees whom the business is in desperate need of. The solution for that dilemma is to be proactive as stated before and to adopt the approach of recruitment marketing as the ultimate solution to generate a qualified pool of candidates through which we can choose whenever we are in need to hire someone. Today we are in a people business and it's no longer about how much you can control the elements of your value chain. In principle, there is no problem with doing this but doing it as the only goal of your business won't consider the people part. The goal for you is to bring the right people into your organisation and they will do on your behalf what needs to be done. It's necessary now more than ever to make the balance between people and business and in some cases peoples' interests are of more priority than other business elements so it's an invitation for you whether you were HR generalist or recruiter to support your business through bringing to your play field the brightest people and more importantly the people who can withstand your values. This a reaffirmation that handling the recruitment in that way will bring more value to you as a person and to your HR function in its strategic transformation journey.

Recruitment Essentials

Before going into the essentials of the recruitment function I want first to highlight briefly on the structural intricacies of that function, these could include the number of people who work within the function, the job roles distinction for these people, the process flow of the function in addition to many other factors.

As a rule of thumb, no two recruitment functions are the same even in two similar organisations. There are many factors that determine the scope and/or complexity and the structure of that function like the nature of the industry. (In consultation companies recruiters must have a high level of consultative-based evaluation skills like administering psychometric assessments for such candidates while in industrial company recruiters must possess the common evaluation skills like mastering the behavioural questioning technique) but the most influential factors in shaping the recruitment function are the size of the organisation and the strategy that the organisation follows. Testing and evaluating candidates in large size organisations depends largely on technology automation for the current tests available while in small size organisations paper-based tests are more common more than on-line tests. The other issue that is affected by size is the headcount of the recruitment function, in big organisations recruitment is a separate function that has multiple recruitment specialists who report to a recruitment manager while in small organisations the number of recruiters is relatively small and there are no recruitment specialists and the HR manager is the person in charge for that function.

When it comes to the organisational strategy the story is different. Many companies are still doing the recruitment without paying attention to the organisational strategy and its reflection on the departmental level, here we jeopardise again the HR-organisational alignment principle, e.g. if your after sales manager is aiming for more engagement for their customers by providing them with a new technology that will detect the failures in their machines beforehand then your goal as a recruiter is to hire candidates who have a high level of the consultation selling skills, which means they must have the ability to assess the customer current situation and matching their needs to the new technology. Before all of that they must have a high level of relationship building skills all over the road. If you hired a highly technical oriented sales people who don't have the needed soft skills then the after-sales manager strategy will be hampered.

Recruitment structure as stated above is changeable and this change in the structure is linked to many factors. The most important thing to be aware ahead of time the moment when the change in the structure is a must, otherwise the business continuity is at big risk if the workforce needs are not met.

Workforce Requirements: Is It Numbers Only?

It has been said long time ago by the great Greek philosopher Plato that "A good decision is based on knowledge and not on numbers." In identifying the workforce requirements for our organisations, we must follow this principle.

We mentioned before that the traditional recruitment function had a big focus on filling the organisational vacancies in terms of the numbers needed only. This would leave us doing a transactional recruitment activity that put on our shoulders a big burden when things go out of control. We face big dilemmas when the new hires' competence levels are not examined carefully. The consequences are very bad on the business, the line managers' goals are hindered, the customers are upset because of the inability of the new customer service officers to solve their problems and above all of that the level of moral for the old timers are very bad especially when they know that their new colleagues are getting higher salaries than they get and their performance level is lower. The risks are magnified when these new hires make big mistakes that cost the business a lot of money and the recruitment team is the first party to be blamed for these mistakes.

In order to avoid these traps, we must adopt a more strategic collaborative recruitment approach, by that I mean that recruiters must possess the needed knowledge of their business lines to be able to identify the required workforce needs as it serves the business demands in terms of the quantity and quality. Here the business acumen competency plays again a key role in differentiating the recruiters and enabling them to make better hiring decisions that support the business. This is one important area of the strategic side of recruitment (the other strategic areas of recruitment will be explored in the subsequent sections). The other important issue is the collaboration between the recruiters and the line managers in identifying the workforce needs. This collaboration is at its best when the line mangers are at year end doing the workforce analysis. My own experience reflects two situations; in the first one the line managers provide their estimation of the needed workforce by collecting the needed numbers from their subordinates without involving HR. In this case HR is an add-on function and the results are a mediocre recruitment yield. The outcome of such an approach is an abundant workforce that increases the human capital cost without any noticeable effect on the organisational bottom line results and overall performance. The other situation is when recruitment function submits its estimation on the workforce needs without involving the other party (the line managers). It is the opposite form the previous situation; here, HR has a presence but it's still isolated which is in conflict with the needed integration between HR and other departments. Someone could argue how it could be possible that recruitment enforces the workforce estimation without involving the line managers. This would be possible and I will explain it through introducing the following real case that happened with me during my tenure with Jordan Tractor & Equipment Company.

It happened that my company went through a bad financial situation that was the result of a country wide-scale economic downturn. At that time, it was crucial to determine if the current workforce size was suitable to the business needs especially with the bad economy shedding its lights on company. We had many meetings at the executive level trying to figure out how to solve this dilemma and most of the opinions focused on making arbitrary workforce cuts. Again, I saw this situation as an opportunity to step in and to show my HR competence and how I can relate it to the organisational business problems. I told my manager that I can do some analysis that will lead to a more scientific approach to workforce estimation. I was talking about the regression analysis (it is a statistical process aimed at estimating the relationship between two variables). My goal was to contribute to the business talk with a more valid and robust analysis-based approach. The variables within this situation were the headcount and the revenue figures for seven years period as stated in Figure 5.

Figure 5 – Regression Analysis

Year	*Revenue*	*No of Employees*
2010	33000042	128
2011	26000392	141
2012	35000661	146
2013	41000667	163
2014	60000366	190
2015	72000074	207
2016	44000615	201
2017	*36000000*	*154.17*

SUMMARY OUTPUT

Regression Statistics

Multiple R	0.845402424
R Square	0.714705259 *Should be close to 100%*
Adjusted R Square	0.657646311
Standard Error	18.39765422
Observations	7

ANOVA

	DF	SS	MS	F	Significance F
Regression	1	4239.6316	4239.631597	12.525735	0.016577172
Residual	5	1692.3684	338.4736806		
Total	6	5932			

	Coefficients	Standard Error	t Stat	P-value	Lower 95%	Upper 95%
Intercept	95.07611237	21.746512	4.372016669	0.0072084	39.17492398	150.9773
Revenue	1.64136E-06	4.638E-07	3.5391715	**0.0165772**	4.49202E-07	2.834E-06

Should be less than 0.05 < 0.05

The first thing I did was to go through a YouTube tutorial to gain better understanding on how to conduct the regression analysis, it was not so difficult to apply it if you just follow the general guidelines on how to read the key indicators of the final result of the analysis, you don't have to be a statistics expert to understand the regression analysis. Within the context of this book I will not go into the details of that analysis because what I did from reading and analysing the data was a personal effort. In ideal case you need to have someone who is an expert in doing such analysis. After getting a positive result from that analysis (the revenue figures in this case were predictive of the number of needed employees) the first thing that came to my mind was to go instantly to my executive managers and tell them that a RIF (Reduction in Workforce) was required. Following that approach would have put me under the isolated HR status mentioned before. I do confess that I had a tendency to follow that approach but after I have reflected on the analysis, I figured out two important things:

1. To base my decisions only on numbers would deprive me from the human factor that constitute the differentiator between a weak and well-thought decision. At the end of day numbers don't consider the other non-quantitative aspects of any decision that if were abandoned then the results are definitely distorted and won't represent the reality as it should be so it was very important to add the needed context to have a complete picture.
2. The other important thing was to bring out HR from the isolation mode from the other functions in my organisation. Allowing for a one-way approach regarding this analysis would increase the gap between HR and other functions, especially that the outcomes of such a decision will impact all the departments widely.

So accordingly, I decided that I must share the results of this analysis with the key stakeholders in my company from bottom up. I first sat with the line managers and gathered their feedback on the business landscape till end of that year, after that I went to the executive management and sought their overall opinions on the business in terms of the expected opportunities.

The result was in the opposite direction of what I found from the analysis; the majority of the managers didn't support the downsizing alternative. They were sure that many opportunities were about to come and these opportunities are of utmost importance to the business and will have a very positive effect on the business, they are make or break deals and if not tapped in instantly then the downsize was inevitable. We decided that the current workforce shouldn't be reduced or else our operational ability to undertake the new opportunities will be undermined. This decision bore also a lot of risks but it was worthy to take that risk because the dividends were attractive. And indeed, our decision not to downsize was the right thing to do as the business opportunities we had after that justified the workforce size in the company.

I will give another example on the importance of the collaborative workforce analysis in an easy way to prove again how important it is to build this collaboration. I recall clearly when a service supervisor came to my office asking to hire five technicians to support the business expansion at that time.

The first thing I did was to request him to fill out the ERF (Employment Requisition Form) that we were using for new hires request. The form is illustrated in Figure 6.

Figure 6 – Employment Requisition Form

Objective:
To make sure that the request is in line with the department and/or company goals and budget, and to assist the HR department in filling the vacant position in due time.

Date of request:	Date new hire needed:............No of vacancies:
	Department:
Job title:	

Job Requirements

Job specification (Knowledge and Skills)	
Education	
Work experience	
Other Requirements	
Tasks, Duties and Responsibilities	

Justification for the Position

If the vacancy is being requested due to increased workload in your department, mention below why your current workforce is not sufficient   ....

If the vacancy is being requested because of new expansion in the business, mention below the reasons for this expansion and why a new hire is needed   ....   Are there any alternative ways available to support your workload volumes and/or business expansion needs without the need to hire additional staff   ....

Approvals

Department Manager: ....   _____Date: Human Resources Manager: ....   _____Date   General Manager: ....   _____Date:

The first two sections (the objective and the job requirements) are standard information that you can find in many ERFs, the main difference and addition to this form lies in the section titled "The Justification for the Position." It contains three questions that are crafted in a straightforward way in order to elicit as much information as possible that are pertinent to the same topic.

The first question investigates the workforce request from the angle of the increasing workload, we ask that question in order to go into the details of the departmental operations and how it's being handled. Most of the answers we got especially from this section were the following. "Yes, we have high demands in our department and we need to hire extra personnel." While, in fact, the situation was totally different when we analysed further.

The second question gives an opportunity for the manager to distinguish between normal business pressures that could seem as an expansion and the real expansion that results in big changes to the way of how operations are being handled and most importantly how job roles are being distributed among current employees and what new skills are needed in terms of the new expansion.

The third question and the most important one is thought provoking; the goal of this question is to urge the managers to think of new ways that could help in avoiding the new hire request. It was very difficult in most of the cases to reach to that question successfully. Answering such a question required a high level of proficiency in the business operations and a creative mind that could come up with a creative solution which were missing elements in most of the managers that I met.

The goal of these three questions was to highlight on the new hires request in a simple way. They are simple in the way they are drafted but the outcome of answering these questions is not simple at all.

Going back to the previous example of the service supervisor and as stated below will prove how valuable it is to answer these questions in an objective way that separates the emotions from taking side when making hiring decisions.

In our case the supervisor was in charge of the preventative maintenance contracts signed with the company customers. The main goal of this function was to visit the customers according to a pre-arranged schedule and to inspect their equipment in order to prevent any expected future failure.

This supervisor was determined that he needed the five technicians and that business will be jeopardised if they weren't hired. After few minutes of talking with him about the current situation of his department I realised that the problem was merely a lack of the right judgment on how to allocate the business volume to his current staff. I noticed also that there could be a need to hire technicians but definitely the number he requested (five technicians) was overly estimated. The first question was the key to begin the discussion. I gave the supervisor the time to talk about his need and the obstacles he was facing with his customers, mainly the customers were outraged because of not visiting them on time as per the service contracts. Without going into the details of the situation the first thing the supervisor asked for was to hire new technicians and usually this is the same scenario I have faced over and over with most of the managers I have worked with.

Again, my business knowledge in the company internal operations (Business Acumen Competency) helped me a lot in resolving this situation. In the following points I will illustrate how we resolved this issue:

1. I asked the supervisor to prepare a list of the contracts the company had then after having it completed, we estimated the number of hours the technician needed in order to make the equipment inspection per visit.
2. Then we calculated the total number of hours needed to cover the customer list within a year time frame (Number of customers * Number of visits * Number of hours per visit).
3. We calculated also the annual number of the actual hours (Productivity rate) the technician could yield after deducting the lost hours.
4. Finally, we divided the total number of hours for the customers' annual visits by the technician annual productivity rate, the end result was the number of technicians needed.

This example reemphasises that knowledge is more important than numbers when making workforce hiring decisions. Referring to our example it was more important to know how the department was functioning rather than just taking the numbers for granted.

Indeed "A good decision is based on knowledge and not on numbers." – Plato

Searching for Talent

The war for talent! It's a concept that we've heard for a long time to the degree that we are obsessed with it, that we don't mention recruitment without linking this concept with it. If we look at it from a practical point of view, we can attest that it's really true. But attesting its validity should not undermine our ability to search for talent effectively and relentlessly.

Searching for talent has been a daunting challenge since decades and many companies are facing dilemmas in their recruiting effectiveness when it comes to hiring on time. The war for talent has made us hopeless so that we don't intensify our efforts when we search for talent, we believe that the most powerful companies with the most elegant brands are the ones that job seekers go after. To some extent it's true but not totally true, there is always a place in your company for the most talented employees in the marketplace as long as you are providing the baseline (competitive rewards, good working conditions, friendly work environment…etc.) that would enable you to attract them. What we need to do when searching for talent is to focus our efforts in attracting the best qualified candidates who really want to join your company. But how we can accomplish that? This could be accomplished through many strategies. One of the most powerful strategies to follow is to build a talent pool through which we can get back to when we are in need to hire. But what usually does it take to build that talent pool?

Establishing and nurturing a talent pool is not an easy job at all; in fact, I believe it's one of the most difficult aspects of HR functions. It's not a reward program through which you have the control on how to be designed and rolled out (of course the design should be based on employees' opinions and demands), it's much more complicated than that. When it comes to candidates sourcing you need to be aware that you are contacting people whom you want to sell your organisation to even if the organisation is well known in the market. It becomes more difficult to attract candidates in such a case because their level of expectations is high, this is one of the challenges that you might face. In my company (Jordan Tractor & Equipment Company) the brand efforts we put in the years 2013 through 2015 were extensive, the goal was to increase the yield rate of candidates who apply to the organisation. Before that the rate of the people who applied to the company was very low and it was a real struggle to find candidates (I didn't say qualified candidates) who are interested to join the company. But after a planned brand effort the results were tremendous, we increased the number of walk-in and online candidates 15-fold within a two years' timeframe. But this achievement didn't solve the problem of attracting the best candidates to join the company. Our company in terms of the rewards benchmark with the market was not the best; other companies were paying relatively higher compensation than us.

Our bet in all of our brand efforts (I will go into detailed explanation about brand strategy later on) was on the following three points:

1. The brand global identity (the company was a caterpillar dealer) and the diverse cultural exposure the company was providing in terms of the continuous contact with caterpillar representatives and the unique training opportunities abroad the home country.
2. The collaborative leadership style that was dominant in the company; leadership was shared rather than imposed, and this has led to more learning opportunities.
3. The team spirit that was dominant in the company which contributed to more collaboration and a friendly working atmosphere.

Following through these brand elements was a critical factor in supporting the talent pool creation, we relied heavily on these elements rather than focusing solely on the C&B side which was not a traction factor by itself. But here lies the main controversy. Are these brand elements considered a change factor in the whole brand efforts? Yes, they are, but they must be derived from your culture, they must be a real reflection on your day-to-day work life. We can talk endlessly about a unique work environment that we aspire to have and accordingly we can elicit from these talks tens of brand ideas but they don't count unless you are living them. You can have two or three main strengths upon which you build your brand identity and that's all what you need to have. A key few positive elements that you really have are more than enough when it comes to brand strategy.

I have witnessed many recruiters who promote for their organisations without realising the brand identity that they already have; in such a case the promotional talks revolve mostly on the direct side of the rewards that the company is offering. Here the result of these promotional campaigns is not optimistic. The recruiters are talking over and over through the job fairs the same talks they had dozens of times without any noticeable change in the recruitment yielding ratios. Of course, nothing will change following that way. But the most dangerous problem is when recruiters fail to attract the talent, they seek to bring on board and begin to talk unrealistically about benefits and things they don't have into their organisation.

Recruiters who follow that approach are not aware of the negative consequences they bring to their organisational brand, candidates who are converted into employees will be shocked once they are onboard and especially when they don't see the things they were told about happening on the ground. A key rule here that recruiters and HR professionals should follow is that **Branding begins from within.** Most of the successful organisations with the big brands have a highly engaged workforce. They spend a lot of time and money on enhancing their work environments in order to retain their current employees. They are true believers that a happy workforce will definitely be the vital link to the outside. Candidates will want to join your organisation when they hear good things about working in your organisation. Social media and the advancement in the communication technology has made it very easy to know how one organisation treats its employees, even tiny details could be exposed easily and shared between a big segment of job seekers, so it has become very important for you as an HR professional to preserve a high engagement level within your organisation and in turn preserving your brand image.

All the previous efforts are of no benefit to you unless you maintain the talent pool you created, allowing it to thrive and be abundant. Maintaining the momentum of this talent pool requires a continuous communication with the candidates' communities who are relevant to your job needs. It's like a marketing strategy that take into account the continuous interaction with the customers as long as the company is operating as should be. Did you hear before that the marketing team in your organisation stopped its promotion for the company products because the sales targets have been met. Of course not, they will persist on their marketing efforts to achieve more. It's the same way in recruiting. You need to keep in touch with your candidates as long as the company is operating. But here there is a precaution. In recruiting there is always a line that you can't pass. It's the line when your recruitment needs are being met. It's very rational to stop your recruitment efforts once you have achieved your goals but how do you continue keeping in touch with candidates even after reaching your goals.

I recall how we once participated in the biggest job fair in my country despite that we were going through a very bad economic situation and we didn't have recruitment needs that could justify our participation. At certain point we didn't want to participate in that job fair moving from an economical point of view, we don't want to waste our money on a recruitment marketing event that wouldn't bring the expected returns. But after we analysed the situation, we had many threats that we wanted to avoid:

1. Stopping the participation in the job fair would deprive us from adding to our talent pool which will disrupt a four-year effort we exerted in building a very competitive talent pool.
2. Not to participate in that job fair would tag us negatively especially since we had consecutive four years participation. Candidates would think twice before thinking to apply to our company, fearing that the company is no longer able to survive.

This decision was the right one to take because after participating I realised how very dangerous it could be if we didn't participate. One of the big companies I knew that was a key participant in the job fair didn't participate that year. I faced many job seekers who asked me personally about why this company didn't participate, the impressions I got from these people confirmed my suspicions also about the reason why a big company is not participating in the biggest job fair in the country.

My goal was to be honest with the candidates and I made it clear for the job seekers who visited our booth that we don't have currently any job vacancies but having a clear understanding about our company and the expected revenue for the near future made me confident about introducing the expected vacancies that would arise when the performance of the company would pick up. The result of this honest integration with the candidates in the job fair was excellent, the number of the people who applied on our recruitment portal also increased.

Still important to mention that talent pools are not only external, they are also internal. In such cases you rely on your employees and especially the talented ones as a recruitment source, like if you promote someone to a hire position. This area will be covered in subsequent sections as part of the succession management issue.

Finally it's very important in order to win the talent for ware to equip ourselves with the brand tools that I mentioned before as the ultimate tool to engage more candidates to apply to your talent pool, and remember that engaging candidates from the outside is a long bridge that you build gradually, starting from inside your organisation.

Competency-Based Selection

Selecting candidates is one of the trickiest areas in recruiting, its difficulty lies in that it's both art and science. It's a science because most of the selection in these days is done through systematic ways, like having a competency standard through which the recruiter can build his/her interview questions. Another systematic approach to build your selection upon is the psychometric assessment tools that are so predictive of the future job performance in terms of the behavioural tendency of the person and how it affects the working environment. On the other side it's an art because the recruiter is making the selection decision based on information gathered from multiple stages of the selection cycle with no reference on how to analyse the data in a meaningful format in order to make a selection decision.

Let's imagine that you were going through a selection process for a marketing manager. In the first stage you screened out their resume from a batch of ten resumes in addition to another two resumes, during the interviews you discovered that they had an extensive experience in market research and you needed someone with such a skill to help in promoting your new launched product but their product knowledge was not so strong as they came from a different industry. The other two candidates had an excellent product knowledge because they came from similar industry but they didn't have the needed market research skill.

At this point it was so difficult for you to choose who is the best fit for your position and your company. You moved further into the selection process by conducting in-tray exercise with a big focus on strategic thinking skill, the first candidate with the market research skill got a lower score compared to the other two candidates. As a recruiter you had to take a decision that is in favour of your organisation and in this case, it was difficult to take a decision with that mix of inconsistent experiences and skills. But keeping in mind that your marketing director has focused so much on market research when he filled out the employment requisition form gave you the insight on the best decision to take.

Taking into account the urgency to establish for new markets for the new product gave you the reason to choose the candidate with the market research skill because the other two candidates didn't have proven skill record with regard to this skill although they had a higher score in the strategic thinking skill compared with the first candidate. The marketing director had a high level of strategic thinking skill and so it was not a big issue if our chosen candidate was a little bit weak in this skill. The marketing director would compensate for the weakness of your candidate regarding this skill and a robust development plan would solve the issue on the mid-term.

So, in recruitment there is no one-size-fits-all approach for all your vacancies, going back to the previous example of selecting the marketing manager we can imagine another scenario in which the marketing director was searching for someone with a high level of strategic thinking skill. In this scenario the product has surpassed the immaturity stage and is now well matured after several years of consistent and big efforts. At this stage it has become vital to find new strategies that will enable the product to develop as per the endless consumer demands and the high competition in the marketplace. So, choosing the candidate with the exceptional market research skills will not be enough in this case, a high strategic management acumen is more needed at this stage in order to make a difference with the current product the company has. Definitely the marketing director will prefer to choose between the other two candidates with the strategic management skills. This was an illustration of the how recruitment is being envisioned as an art.

Now the most important question to ask here, how can we make a competency-based interview? Let's first define the word competency. Competency comprises KSAOs (knowledge, skills, abilities and other characteristics). The definition of these elements is illustrated below:

1. Knowledge: is the body of information you need to acquire for certain competency.
2. Skills: is the proficiency level in applying the knowledge.
3. Abilities: your ability to demonstrate the knowledge and the skills in a given situation successfully.
4. Other characteristics: are the other traits and/or job requirements that are not core to the main competency but would complement it in certain areas (They don't fall under KSAs).

In order to make it clearer what is the meaning of competency I will explain the communication competency against the above elements (KSAOs).

1. The knowledge side in communication is about how the person is well-versed about the elements of the communication process; in this case they are the sender, the message, the receiver, and the feedback.
2. The skill side of the communication competency could be the active listening, usually a well-known approach that we convey to our employees when coaching them on the effective communication is the LISTEN technique as illustrated in Figure 7.
3. The ability to deliver effective communication could be the person's ability to persuade another person with her point of view.
4. Other characteristics could be your awareness of specific industry terminology that would facilitate your understanding in a communication situation, e.g. to know that the AFA (Applied Failure Analysis) is a technical terminology that is about the technician's ability to diagnose the reasons for certain spare parts failure.

Figure 7 – LISTEN Approach

L	Look interested
I	Involve yourself by responding
S	Stay on target
T	Test your understanding
E	Evaluate the message
N	Neutralize your feelings

After we have defined the meaning of competency we will move now to the way how competency-based questions are being formulated. In competency-based questions we focus on discovering the behavioural side of the candidate during the interview by asking about past experiences he/she went through. Human beings rarely change and thus their past behaviour is the same as it would be at the present and most probably will remain the same in the future. The most common approach that recruiters use when asking competency-based questions is the STAR approach as illustrated in Figure 8.

Figure 8 – Star Approach

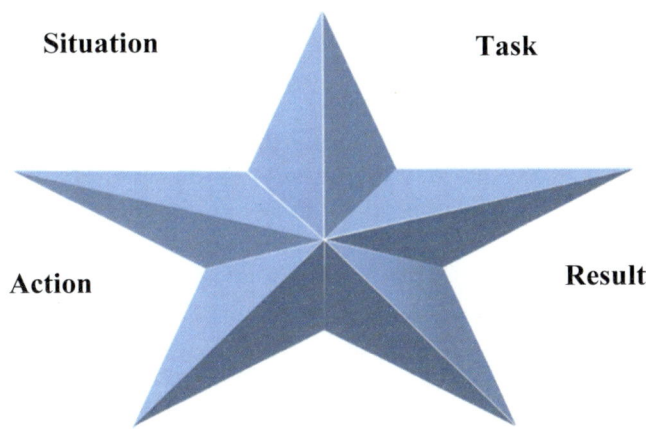

Situation   Task

Action   Result

This approach helps you as recruiter to examine the competency mastery for the candidates whom you are interviewing. The most important element is to ask about past real situations that the candidates experienced, be careful of asking hypothetical interview questions, like if you ask the candidate, what would you do if faced resistance from your subordinates when implementing new initiative? Such questions are very risky and they don't lead you to where you want to reach. Candidates always give you the answer you want to hear. But when asking them, tell me about a situation when you faced resistance from your subordinates when you implemented new initiative? The outcome is definitely more positive, candidates mostly can't create fake situations as it's very easy to notice that they are lying so here you have the opportunity to discover the targeted competency.

Before giving an example on how to use this technique I want to make it clear that this approach is not a stand-alone technique in the selection process, it's a key part of the selection process but there should be other elements that would support you selection decision like using online tests for certain jobs in addition to the competency-based questions.

This approach helps you to be more objective when selecting candidates because you are asking job related questions and mostly you are not relying on your intuition. I will not discuss the human biases that would sabotage even the most well-designed interviews as it's a comprehensive topic that must be left to people who are specialists in such areas but I will talk briefly about some common mistakes that we do during the interview process:

1. Overlapping during the interview which means that the recruiter shifts between irrelevant subjects which could distract the candidate and thus create an atmosphere of stress, an example would be that the recruiter was asking about the time management competency and suddenly while the candidate was talking about a past situation he had with arranging a project deliverables the recruiter jumped to ask about the training background for that candidate which resulted in cutting the candidate's talk and thus not receiving the full idea of that competency.
2. Lack of documentation which would result in inaccurate picture about the candidate's overall interview evaluation. This area is very tricky because writing the details during the interview will again distract the candidate and could give the impression that you are not excreting the needed courtesy toward the candidate by giving your full attention to that candidate. An advice that we give to recruiters during the interview is to write key words when the candidate is talking about herself, like if the candidate talked about her excellent negotiation skills with the suppliers in getting better prices when purchasing the maintenance tools. You can write (Negotiation / company supplies) as a guiding note that you won't miss any important information as long as you are following up on your notes directly once you finish your interview. Taking longer time to review your notes in order to elaborate them more would definitely affect the validity of your details and thus your judgement.
3. Brief interview vs. excessive interview, not giving the needed time for the candidate to talk about him/herself will lead to insufficient information about the candidate's overall evaluation, conversely talking too much in the interview could yield unneeded information which might confuse the recruiter to make the proper judgement. It's always advisable to strike a balance during the interview, not talking too much or too little. And one of the golden rules when it comes to interviewing candidates is to listen more than you talk. It's the candidate whom you want to discover and not yourself.

Once again, the interview and selection pitfalls are numerous but the aforementioned interview mistakes are the ones I have encountered at early stages of my career and they had a negative impact on the selection process at that time. Here I will stress again the importance of leveraging your awareness in the human psychological barriers that could affect your overall judgement to select the right candidate. I mentioned before that I will not go deep into that area as I prefer to leave to the specialists, but it's worth mentioning a case that I faced during my career that would give the reader a glimpse on what it means to overcome the trap of interview errors.

I remember once when I was interviewing several candidates for a safety officer position when one of them entered my office with his gloomy face and harsh voice. At first, I got the impression that this guy was inflexible and his overall appearance was not encouraging to move forward with him. But after few seconds I reconsidered the whole issue and decided to give him a fair opportunity as for everybody else.

After going through a complete and effective interview the result really amazed me, the guy was very knowledgeable about a wide range of safety issues in addition to a proven track record for past successful experiences. He was the best one for this job! After I completed the rest of the interviews, he was the one who was selected for this position. In the HR technical knowledge, we call this mistake the first impression error and if I didn't question my initial judgment at that time the result would have been very bad, the loss of a very qualified candidate who would have been an added-value to the company.

Now getting back to the STAR technique we will give an example on how to ask such questions. You are in the middle of an interview with a potential HR supervisor and one of the key competencies for this position is the consultation competency. You ask the candidates about a past situation when they offered an advice for their management on a key managerial initiative. They are talking about how they introduced a new 360-degree feedback tool as a solution to develop the skills of three supervisors in the marketing department. I will break down the situation against the STAR technique as the following:

- S (Situation): at this stage you ask the candidate about the situation that took place and what exactly it was about. It's preferred to ask the candidate about recent situations as people usually forget the details of old situations and details are very important in competency-based questions.
- T (Task): here you need to know exactly what was the role of the candidate in this situation. In our example, it would make a big difference if the HR supervisor didn't suggest the solution and just executed the idea of the 360-degree feedback tool vs. if the idea was theirs.
- A (Action): you need to know here if the HR supervisor had a detailed action plan to roll out the initiative. You might ask them if they had a direct role in the execution vs. if the department manager excreted that role, you might ask them if they had a role in designing the individual learning plan for the marketing supervisors or not.
- R (Result): this is the most important element of the STAR technique; here you need to hear a positive outcome as result of the past details. It won't benefit you to hear all the previous talk from the HR supervisor explaining what they have done to discover that neither the marketing supervisors nor the marketing manager have taken the advice of the HR supervisor regarding the learning plan, it's an indication that something went wrong and that you need to know what it was.

But there is an exception to that rule. Sometimes you deliberately ask the candidate about situations with negative outcome. In our past example you ask the HR supervisor about the same situation but we assume here that the HR supervisor was not successful in the solution they introduced. Of course, you were planning for this question from the beginning, like asking, "Tell me about a past situation when you offered an advice for your management on a key managerial initiative but you weren't successful?"

The answer you expect is not to hear a reaffirmation that the HR supervisor didn't succeed in their proposal. What you want to hear is that they tried again with new modifications to the original initiative or even with introducing new different initiative until they succeeded in their pursuit. In other words, you were probing the perseverance competency.

Another key note to have a complete and successful competency-based interview is your concentration on the key job competencies, you can't ask a salesperson on the analytics competency (Although an important competency but not a critical success factor to the sales job) and not to ask her about the key competencies needed for a successful job performance like the negotiation skills. The competency-based interview is job related and in order to be consistent in your competency-based approach you should have a valid document or reference for every job when you are planning for this kind of interviews. Job descriptions are very important as a reference to elicit from the needed competency-based questions as long as you relate them with applicable and recent competency frameworks or catalogues. If you don't have such valid documents you can refer to shrm.org website for job description documents that you can build upon them.

Competency-based selection as stated earlier is a key approach to examine the candidates' current proficiency level in certain competencies, and it's important to make sure that you complement this approach with other selection tools in order to have many perspectives which will support your final decision whether to select or to discard a candidate.

Finally, it's of utmost importance to know that whatever selection approach you use you will never reach a 100% accurate selection decision, all of what we do when it comes to selection is to enhance the predictability of our decisions. It would not be so effective to rely solely on competency-based interview for a vehicle technician and not to make the technical tests to evaluate the technical competency which could be a make or break factor in such a case. But nevertheless, even if that technician had a high-test score in both the competency-based and the technical tests it doesn't mean that he will succeed in his job. There could be other factors that that could cause the failure of the most talented employees. The work environment could be destructive which could lead to a high turnover rate with the newcomers. In such a case the employee's individual competence has no direct effect on the person's success or failure. But that wouldn't suppress the effectiveness of the competency-based interview as a vital approach for a better selection decision. The number one differentiator for the organisation's success is its employees and thus selecting the most talented and effective employees is the only way for an effective and profitable organisation.

Onboarding

Before talking about onboarding I want to highlight on a very important note within the context of this chapter and in turn the whole book. Recruitment is a very comprehensive topic that has a lot of intricacies and so I didn't go into that deep level of complication because this book is dedicated to entry-level HR professionals and it is also helpful for early mid-level HR professionals who are still acquiring the SHRM BOCK (Body of Competency and Knowledge).

The details of the recruitment operational activities are easy to attain, you can for example download the ERF (Employment Requisition Form) from many websites but mostly it won't provide you with the hands-on experience you will find in this book, so I tried as much as possible to equip the reader with the vital issues that really make a difference in the day-to-day work rather than focusing on easy attainable recruitment details and forms. Nevertheless, I will talk later on in this chapter about general recruitment policy so it would help you as a starting point for further investigation as per your organisational needs.

This idea of focusing on a very few strategic elements that would save you valuable time is replicated in all the chapters of this book and by digesting them carefully you definitely will be able to build the strategic acumen competency, and thus applying the four levels of HR model effectively.

Now let's talk about onboarding. This concept has been a hot topic lately as it's tackling a very sensitive issue, how to retain our newly hired talent with focusing on accelerating their productivity within the shortest time possible.

Onboarding as a concept is an HR practice that extends the orientation (usually a process that last for few days through which the company introduces the newcomers to their colleagues and their office area with a little bit focus on some of the rules and the regulations of the company) traditional process for a longer period. The essence of the onboarding is to equip the new comers with the needed knowledge and skills so they are aware of what's needed of them so they can achieve their deliverables within the shortest time possible. The most important area that usually takes a big deal of the onboarding is the organisational cultural awareness for the new comers which is an overlooked area in many onboarding programs, will talk about it later on.

It was proven through many studies that the biggest risk when it comes to turnover rate is the new hires dropout rate. New hires at their early career stage leave their companies in the first six months while the more experienced new hires, let's say the mid-level career professionals, leave their companies within the first 18 months.

The onboarding practice didn't emerge overnight, it has deep roots through many interrelated HR processes. The high cost that some companies incurred while recruiting their top talent and then losing them has been one of the major reasons that made these companies searching for solutions for such dilemma. The unplanned training that consumes a lot of hours for the new comers with no concrete outcomes has made the issue more complicated and thus reemphasising the need for a robust solution. Most importantly the need to achieve the newcomers' assimilation into the organisational culture had its most significant effect on expanding the traditional orientation programs.

The solution for the previous problems was to intensify the orientation practice with more well-thought actions that would result in a more systematic and consistent practice that ultimately would tackle the new comers turnover problem. This practice as we know now is onboarding.

Onboarding systems are well spread all over the world and they are easily accessible but it's not a wise practice to replicate these systems without studying them first and matching them with your organisational needs. The first thing to do before establishing onboarding system is to formulate your onboarding mission. Mission statements reflect what the organisation's main purpose is and what the organisation is doing.

Onboarding mission statement should be a reflection of the main statement. In IT industries for example the focus usually is on leveraging the technical know-how for the new comers because it's a key element in the success or the failure of the IT guy. In customer service-oriented companies like in the telecommunication industries the focus is on advancing the soft skills of the customer service officers in terms of how to deal effectively with difficult customers and most importantly how to satisfy their needs instantly with a high-quality service.

So, an example of onboarding mission statement for an IT company would be the following (we develop highly motivated IT professionals who possess the latest technical IT expertise in their industry). Drafting such a message would guide the onboarding process owners (HR and direct managers) to achieve the onboarding deliverables around that mission, e.g. HR would strive to convince the product development manager to include within their annual budget specific provisions that cover the software licenses for the junior product specialists in order to give them the latitude to apply what they are learning immediately, such a practice would instil a sense of pride for these junior employees as they would feel that they are being taken care of.

After you have designed the onboarding mission statement you need to be aware of the following four elements to be included within your overall onboarding system. They are called the four Cs (SHRM Foundation's Effective Practice Guidelines Series – **Onboarding New Employees: Maximizing Success**[1]) and they are:

1. **Compliance:** is the lowest level and includes teaching employees basic legal and policy-related rules and regulations.
2. **Clarification:** refers to ensuring that employees understand their new jobs and all related expectations.
3. **Culture:** is a broad category that includes providing employees with a sense of organisational norms – both formal and informal.

---

[1] Talya N. Bauer, Ph.D. Onboarding New Employees: Maximizing Success). SHRM Foundation, 2010.

4. **Connection:** refers to the vital interpersonal relationships and information networks that new employee must establish.

These four elements don't necessarily have to be designated in separate sections within your onboarding system. Your onboarding system must revolve around them, in other words, the outcome of your onboarding system must be the end result of these four elements.

Let's focus on the element number three, Culture, as an example. It's an important segment of the whole process that must be designed during the onboarding period (usually lasts from 6 months to one year depending on the nature of the organisation and the complexity of the job role for the new comers). The purpose of this stage is to make the new comers feeling included within their new work environment in the shortest time possible and this won't be achieved unless it was planned for since the beginning of the process.

We can add to the direct manager onboarding to do list that the new comer must be introduced to the his/her colleagues regularly in formal and informal meetings that will help the new comer in knowing the team members closely and regularly. This is a practice that can make the socialisation of the new comer to the work environment easier and faster.

Another professional practice is to guarantee that the direct manager is reviewing the code of ethics with the new employee at every stage of the onboarding period to make sure that the employee is being involved within the culture rapidly and as listed through the code of ethics. You can't expect the new employee to share her new insights with her team members as stated in the code of ethics if you are not making her aware of the teamwork ethical standards and to reinforce these standards over and over until it becomes part of the employee's daily work habits.

So, these four elements must be embedded within your system. Now we will move to the next segment you need to cover within your onboarding system. We will talk about some important principles that will guide you all over the road of onboarding a new comer, these are:

1. Onboarding is not a one-time event, it's a process that begins before the employee joins the organisation and it lasts for a certain period (six months to one year) until the employee's performance kicks off. Again, onboarding extends the traditional orientation programs for a much longer period.
2. Onboarding success is not the sole responsibility of HR; it's a group effort that includes the HR and the direct manager. Also, the employee has a distinct role in making this planned effort a big success.
3. Onboarding system must be planned for thoughtfully in order to have remarkable results. It should include all the elements that are consistent with the employee job level and experience. You shouldn't include a segment that focuses on cultural integration for a new comer who just graduated recently from the university. You can substitute this segment

by making the employee aware of the code of ethics by introducing him to what's accepted and what's not accepted and gradually you can leverage his cultural intelligence as he is progressing through the first year of his employment. You can begin for example to introduce the concept of cultural awareness assessment tools (GlobeSmart is an example of reference for such tools) for the new comers after the first nine months of employment as a reference they can get back to in order to build more comprehensive awareness on the components of the prevailing culture. By that you can guarantee that the employee is being assimilated smoothly within the culture without any hardships.

Following through the above areas will guarantee for you numerous benefits, of these benefits are:

1. New comers are enormously motivated when they join new companies so taking advantage of this motivation through an effective onboarding experience will contribute dramatically to create a high momentum that will help to achieve the organisational goals.
2. A key benefit that should be directly touched is the decrease in turnover, a well-planned onboarding program will serve that purpose.
3. Another key benefit is the increase of the individual productivity in a relatively short period which will contribute in the overall organisational productivity. Also, savings in waste cost and cost reduction will contribute in the individual productivity.
4. Again, the organisational cultural awareness stage when having onboarding program will be shorter and thus adding to the overall productivity of the organisation.

Now we will talk about the onboarding framework and what should be included within an effective onboarding program. This framework is generic and could be customised as per your needs.

Onboarding usually goes into a sequence of multiple stages. The first stage is mandatory and is a must in any onboarding program, it's what we call the Pre-arrival stage. The second stage is also mandatory but there could be a variation in the sequence of this stage. Usually we call it the **Preparation** stage, it begins from the first day and it could last to one year. The variation in this stage lies in the sequence as I just said. Some companies begin the review with the new employee onboarding plan at the first week and then move forward and make a check-in after the first month, then the first three month, then they do the mid-year review until reaching the first-year review. Other companies might go into a similar sequence but without making the first month review. Others might do a first month review and complete the sequence until reaching the six months review and they stop there.

The final stage is the last step in the onboarding program and we call it the **Onboarding Program Effectiveness**. At this stage the effectiveness of the overall program is captured in a survey format to know the strengths and weaknesses of the program. It's worth mentioning that the end of the onboarding program is just the start of another important stage of the employee's career life. Taking care of the employee is a continuous cycle that begins with every new intervention the employee goes through and it won't stop unless the employee decides to leave the company. Which means that onboarding as examined from a broader perspective is part of every stage of the employees' life work with varying degrees and intensity. An employee at his/her mid-career stage need a special intervention than the early-career employee when it comes to coaching. Employee with more maturity need more advanced work projects to progress within their career with little interference from their direct manager, while an employee with less maturity and experience needs less advanced work projects with more interference from the direct manager.

Now we will examine the onboarding stages in more detail. The first stage (The Pre-Arrival) is very crucial and a lot of the onboarding program success depends largely on this stage. Usually this stage begins almost two weeks prior to the arrival of the new employee. The HR professional at this stage is required to accomplish many to-do items that are very important to be ready before the employee joins the company. A sample of these items is listed below in Figure 9 (Pre-Arrival Checklist).

Figure 9 – Pre-Arrival Checklist

	Work Area	HOD	HR
☐	Assign a workstation/phone extension.	✓	
☐	Establish computer, network, parking pass, and telephone access.	✓	
☐	Order furniture as needed.	✓	
☐	Order office supplies, business cards, mobile phone.	✓	
☐	Ensure email set up (with access or password).	✓	✓
☐	HR software access.		✓
☐	Obtain items with logo or brand to give on first day as welcome gift.		✓
☐	Create a key list of people and employees that the new employee should meet and interview to get a broader understanding of their roles.	✓	
☐	Draft a work and training plan for the new employee's first three to six months.	✓	✓

	Communication	HOD	HR
☐	Welcome email, letter or telephone call to employee after offer is accepted.		✓
☐	Buddy to call the new employee to welcome him/her a few days before the start date.	✓	
☐	E-mail to co-workers and key contacts announcing start date of new employee.	✓	
☐	Organise a welcome gathering.	✓	

The goal of this stage is to make the new employee feel welcomed at his/her new company and to get the impression that company is a professional one which in turn will affect the employment brand effectively. Someone could argue that creating positive impression is not enough and it's considered something superficial. I agree on that statement completely but I believe that creating positive impression from the beginning of the onboarding is very important although not decisive in achieving a complete success. It won't bring a complete motivation to the new employee if a training plan was prepared from the first week but the needed office supplies like having a computer device is not ready yet. So, preparing all what's needed in the pre-arrival checklist will establish for a solid ground for the next stages.

A related example is when we are taking a training workshop with a trainer who is well competent in their subject matter but they weren't successful in grasping the audience's interest at the beginning of the workshop. Some trainees would give the trainer a bad evaluation at the end of the workshop regardless of whether the trainer made a progress through the workshop or not. Most of the times we as human beings are a prey of our own shortcomings. We tend to judge people after the initial impression we get and it lasts for longer periods more than we could imagine. It becomes very difficult to change these perceptions unless something drastic happens that might cause a shift in our thoughts.

It's also very important to clarify the responsibility of both HR and the direct manager. By doing that you are eliminating any blur in the responsibility of both parties and most importantly you reemphasise that onboarding is a mutual responsibility between both HR and the line managers.

Now we will move to the next stage (**The Preparation**). Again, I will give an example of some of the items required to be accomplished at this stage. This stage is the longest one all over the onboarding period and it comprises many sub stages, for the purpose of our example I will list some of the to do items of the first three months checklist, Figure 10.

Figure 10 – First Three Months Checklist

First Three-Month Review	HOD	HR
Meet with employee to review progress on the initial work plan including training and development activities.	✓	✓
Meet with the employee's buddy and / or staff members to review progress on integration into the division/branch/team. Follow-up to resolve any issues.	✓	✓
Follow-up on any questions the employee has regarding HR e.g. pay, benefits, health insurance and social security etc.	✓	✓
Provide employee with a paper copy of the one-year online onboarding evaluation survey so that the employee can consider the points throughout the year. (First Year on Boarding System Effectiveness Survey)	✓	✓

You can notice in the second point from the previous table that I mentioned the word Buddy. It's vital that an experienced employee plays the role of the buddy of the new employee. His/her role is to help the new employee during the onboarding program with the matters that he/she can't explore individually. Such issues could be how to work through the internal procurement procedure or how to deal with the team from day-to-day without making any fractions in the relationship, usually new employees stumble with that area as they don't know the prevailing culture and how to deal properly with the surrounding environment.

The buddy within this context is a safe net for the new employee, he's the mentor who guarantees that the new employee is progressing all over the road without hitting any block. It's important that the choice of the buddy should be based on solid criteria. This person must be willing to take this responsibility voluntarily, he/she must have the necessary mentoring skills and the most important aspect is to have someone who is credible enough to earn the trust of the new employee or else the whole onboarding process is jeopardised. Usually the buddy undertakes the following responsibilities:

1. Contact the new employee before they join the company so they would be introduced to each other.
2. Introduce the new employee to the new team members.
3. Explain office procedures (e.g. dress code policy) as applicable.
4. Explain whom to contact for different issues (e.g. HR for employment related issues).
5. To meet regularly with each other at least for the first three months until the employee's performance has improved.
6. Motivate the new employee as much as possible to encourage him/her to perform at his/her best.

The list could go longer but these are the main responsibilities that the buddy undertakes.

Now come the final stage, the **Onboarding Program Effectiveness**. This stage is very important as it measures the effectiveness of the program and whether it achieved the intended results or not. Below you will see the questions that usually are important to ask about in order to capture any areas of improvement.

Questions	Very Dissatisfied	Dissatisfied	Satisfied	Very Satisfied
All the required resources, tools and support needed were provided to you upon your pre-arrival. (For example, Work station, phone, e-mail, etc.)	1	2	4	4
You felt comfortable and welcomed to the organisation upon your pre arrival.	1	2	3	4
Your Buddy answered all your questions and queries upon pre-arrival.	1	2	3	4
Regular follow up was provided to you continuously throughout the onboarding period by all parties concerned (Buddy, HR, HOD and Co-workers).	1	2	3	4
You had a clear insight of your roles and responsibilities and training program you were assigned.	1	2	3	4

Finally, it's very important to align the system with your organisational strategies and goals continuously. Onboarding at the high peak economic cycle should be accelerated enough in order to get the employee onboard as soon as possible as long as it's not compromising the quality of the program. In high tech companies or companies whose job structure require longer learning curve than others onboarding must be planned carefully and could take longer time than the usual learning programs.

Onboarding if looked at from a strategic perspective would serve the organisational goals in retaining its best acquired talent and to accelerate the productivity needed for the success of the organisation.

Recruitment and Technology

Before I preview the general recruitment policy for your reference I will talk about the importance of technology in recruitment. Adopting new recruitment technology has a big effect on the key recruitment metric (Time to Hire) that we will discuss later on.

We talked about the importance of shifting from the traditional recruitment methods to the modern ones, mainly we talked about recruitment marketing. Any effective marketing function depends largely on market research and market analysis and taking into account the complexity of the new global landscape and the big number of competitors we are witnessing nowadays. It will never work out to use primitive data analysis techniques and tools, modern marketing specialists are using state-of-the-art data analysis software and techniques in order to capture the new business opportunities on the spot and before the competition is aware of any of these opportunities and thus creating a competitive edge, recruitment is not an exception at all.

Effective companies that have strategic HR departments are using the best recruitment technology they could afford in order to facilitate their recruitment activities smoothly and effectively.

The main problem that all the recruiters are facing is the complexity of recruitment procedures and what it takes to reach your goal of hiring the best talent.

Imagine that you're planning to hire four junior auditors for your financial services firm. You begin the process by posting the vacancy on a local job board in your country. After few days you begin exploring the resumes (in certain cases they could reach few hundreds of resumes) you got one by one, you go deeper to examine some resumes carefully for candidates who have professional certifications. After two days you complete the first stage then you go to the next one. You ask the recruitment officer to arrange with the auditing department to do the technical assessment for thirty candidates who were screened out of 120 resumes.

After you have finished the previous stage (the technical assessment which needed three days and dedicated two personnel from HR and the auditing department) you move to the one-on-one interviews with the finalists (ten candidates who passed the assessment). It takes another three days to make the interviews. Before that a big effort was exerted from HR in order to prepare the employment applications for the ten candidates with the technical assessments attached to them. This documentation was sent to the auditing department director to screen them and to give his notes.

Finally, you begin the process of salary negotiation and then sending job offers to the selected four candidates who met all the required criteria. As part of your recruitment procedure you make a phone call with the rest of the candidates who weren't selected. Can you imagine the headache you went through!

Let's reimagine the same scenario but this time with different circumstances. You begin posting the vacancy on a local job board that is linked directly with your career portal. After few days you log into the portal and through the auto filtration feature you enter the employment criteria you need and the system generates in few seconds thirty candidates who meet these criteria. The stakeholders in this process (the auditing director and two HR personnel) who are already identified in the recruitment portal are notified by the ATS (Applicant Tracking System) on the potential thirty candidates who should go through the assessment.

The HR personnel send the on-line test instructions to the thirty candidates after calling them and they get the responses on the tests within one day. Ten candidates who passed the test are notified through the system on the dates for their interviews the day after. The whole process of the test administration and selecting the candidates who passed is completely done through the ATS. Finally, the HR personnel sends an apology letter to the candidates who weren't selected through the system and in turn this vacancy is closed successfully.

Using recruitment technology has saved the HR department a lot of effort and time, in our case the saving was almost half the time. This example reflected a small-scale company and thus the saving couldn't be noticeable just from one vacancy. You need to wait for a one-year period and to calculate the savings for the total vacancies you had, but the effect of the recruitment technology is much more noticeable and has the biggest effect on the HR bottom line operational expenses. In global companies that has tens of thousands of employees one vacancy means also thousands of candidates so using such technology is a must and the savings are enormous. We are talking about the time we save of many HR personnel and the direct managers who are involved in this process. This saving in time if was quantified in monetary terms would equal to a big portion of the money we save from the HR yearly budget and most importantly it would have the biggest impact on the time to hire metric which we will discuss later on.

For the purpose of this book I will talk about the needed features of an effective recruitment portal and the ATS (Applicant Tracking System).

The first step toward acquiring such a system is to make sure that you are really in a big need of this technology. You need to prove to your management that the benefits as compared to the cost can justify the investment. What you need to focus on again is the time that you can save when using this technology and clarifying in a monetary term this value as I stated before. Here you need to have a proper documentation for two major things. The first issue is to track the number of vacancies you had at least for a three-year timeframe. You must show that there is a big increase in the number of vacancies and how it affected the HR department's ability to respond properly to the recruitment needs in your organisation. Secondly you must show the effect of this increase on the time to hire metric (usually a negative effect) and to relate this also to numbers by calculating the cost of unfilled vacancies that I will talk about in the recruitment measurement system.

After that comes the technical features that must be available in the technology you will choose in order to have an effective solution, we will preview them now. The recruitment technology has two complementary parts, the first one is the recruitment portal and it should be linked directly to the company career page. The second one is the ATS (Applicant Tracking System) and it follows the recruitment portal in the sequence of the recruitment process execution.

First of all, we will talk about the features required in your recruitment portal which I would like to call the bucket in which all the resumes you receive are captured and saved for any future reference. These features are the following:

- **Resumes Database:** this feature is very important and is considered the first step that will feed your system with the needed resumes that you can choose from whenever you have any need. Building this database requires a lot of effort and time and it's based mainly on your brand image and the attractiveness you can generate to your career web page. It's vital within this database to have an advance filtration feature as it's going to be the tool that you will use to navigate through the big volumes of resumes whenever you have a vacancy.
- **Vacancy Tracking:** this feature enables you to track the vacancies you had within a specified time frame, it should include the active and the expired vacancies. It helps you a lot to go back to a vacancy you closed recently for several reasons. You could navigate again through the candidates who applied previously to choose from them again in case your first hire has left the company let's say during the first six months. Another benefit you will gain is to support your recruitment metrics dashboard with the needed data, e.g. the number of candidates who applied or who viewed your post but didn't apply is helpful to measure the recruitment yielding ratios.
- **Future Potential Candidates:** this feature is not widely used or known. Within this feature you build special database for candidates who have high potential but not necessarily needed at the time being. Highly progressive recruiters use this approach as part of their CRM (Candidates Relationship Management) strategy. They nurture their recruitment database with highly qualified candidates who could be potential employees one day. This proactive recruitment strategy is very crucial in decreasing the needed time to hire which is a big concern for all the recruiters all over the world. You could choose whatever name you find appropriate for this feature. It could be named High Potential Candidates – Future Reference or Other Folders. The most important thing is to adopt the concept as a part of your recruitment strategy.
- **Recruitment Analytics Dashboard:** this dashboard should complement the previous features and should be integrated with them to extract useful data you can use for more insights on your recruitment effectiveness. It could include the recruitment source analysis (the source that yielded the most qualified candidates), the gender distribution for the candidates who applied to your organisation, the educational background analysis and many more options. These features

mostly are a built-in feature but you can ask the solution provider to customise the software as per your needs.

The aforementioned features were specific to my company but it doesn't mean that they are inclusive, there are dozens of features that can be built within your system that can yield valuable information that you can use to enhance your recruitment effectiveness. At the end of the day you need to justify the thousands of dollars that your company invested in this technology.

Now we will talk about the second part of the recruitment technology that is integral to the first one. It's the ATS (Applicant Tracking System). Within this technology you need to have the following features:

1. **The Vacancies Tab:** this feature enables you to create new vacancies for your organisation that are traceable, which means that the point you create the vacancy till the vacancy is closed should be fully monitored and traced through all the stakeholders. This feature help alleviate the stress and the hardship that accompanies the traditional recruitment procedure that holds a big paper work and admin burden for the recruiters who facilitate the process. It's much easier for a recruiter to search the ATS for certain applications rather than searching manually tens of applications. Also, there are sub features within the vacancies tab that are necessary for an effective recruitment cycle:

   - The vacancy page that is linked with the main career page should include a recruitment action feature that such actions could include the ability to send an email to the department manager notifying her about the candidates who passed the selection test. A feedback form detailing the interview results is also important.
   - The vacancy summary page. It includes the actions that took place regarding any vacancy. These actions might be the HR notes on the applicants who were nominated for the first interview, the notes from the department manager regarding the best candidates who passed the technical interview…etc.
   - The documents tab which is the container for all the related documents during the recruitment process like the candidate resume, the candidate evaluation form…etc.

2. **The Analytics Tab:** this tab should reflect the data pertaining to the number of candidates per vacancy, the number of qualified candidates, the number of events per vacancy which shows the efficiency of the recruitment process in terms of the number of stages per each vacancy (the less the stages the more efficient is the process), the number of generated offers…etc. There should be also another analytics tab that shows the system users activities like the number of users who used the

system in a certain period, the users' commitment to use the system as indicated by the login tracking...etc.

Now comes the most important piece that will complete the whole picture. It's the recruitment process efficiency how it integrates well with the technology solution. It will make no difference if you have the state-of-the-art recruitment technology and your process is not compatible with that technology.

Bill Gates wrote in his book *The Road Ahead* with Nathan Myhrvold and Peter Rinearson; Viking Books, 1995, "The first rule of any technology used in a business is that automation applied to an efficient operation will magnify the efficiency. The second is that automation applied to an inefficient operation will magnify the inefficiency."

In order for a recruitment process to be efficient the stages within the process must be reasonable enough that the time taken to achieve them is not long, also adding unneeded extra steps to the process will result in a lengthy process that will affect the efficiency of the process and thus the time to hire metric. I remember clearly how it was daunting for me in my company (Jordan Tractor) to handle the hiring process of service engineers. Usually the most challenging part was the testing stage for these engineers. They went through the technical theoretical test as per the mother company standards and then the candidates who are successful in this test would go to the second one (practical test that measures the mechanical aptitude for the candidates).

When we applied the recruitment software the efficiency of the process was flawed because of the number of the recruitment stages that were relatively longer than required. The technology didn't help us a lot as the software was accelerating the process that was lengthy. The software was capturing the outcomes of the first testing stage (The Theoretical Test) and then capturing the outcomes of the second stage (The Practical Test) consecutively. Of course, the software helped to accelerate every stage merely (the documentation of theoretical tests and then capturing these tests on the recruitment portal made it very easy for anyone to search through the results without bothering with the complexity of the paper work) but the overall process was not that efficient.

In order to beat that shortcoming, we came out with a key solution that was instrumental for the whole process, we automated the theoretical test through partnering with local tests provider and then we integrated this online test with our recruitment technology. This big achievement helped us to eliminate an important portion of the time needed to complete the testing stages. Previously the candidates had first to submit the theoretical test and then to wait for few days until the results were ready (it was completely a manual process) and then to go through the practical test. After the automation of the test we were able to send the theoretical test through emails to the target candidates so they could submit the test from any place. After they finished the test the results were sent directly to our portal with no single interference from anyone. After that comes the practical test stage which by default must be administered in our company.

In summary, the progress we made in the automation of the online test was really of big value to us and to the investment we made in the recruitment technology. The technology in itself would never had been an added value option if we didn't optimise the recruitment process. So, this is a reaffirmation that an efficient process is the key to the success of any technology implementation.

General Recruitment Policy Guidelines

This section will provide you with the main recruitment guidelines that must be followed in order to have a consistent process across all the departments in any organisation. These guidelines should be conveyed to all the department managers so they are aware of the recruitment process and how to handle any vacancy within the accepted rules of the organisation.

These guidelines aim to clear the responsibility of HR and the department managers regarding the hiring of new personnel. They are the following:

1. **Objective of the Recruitment Policy:** this is a statement that must be stated at the beginning of any recruitment policy, it reflects the purpose of the recruitment policy as related to the organisational mission. Mainly most of the recruitment policies aim at hiring best of the best employees who possess the values of the company. If you are a logistics services company then you need to focus on hiring candidates who have a high level of urgency in responding to the customers' needs. It's also important to highlight in the objective statement on giving equal opportunity for all the candidates who have the needed specifications.
2. **Scope of the Recruitment Policy:** this part of the recruitment policy identifies the target candidates for the available vacancies in your organisation. It has two sides, vacancies for the external candidates and they must go through the traditional hiring procedure. These vacancies mostly pertain to first level jobs up to the supervisory level. The second side covers the vacancies for the internal candidates (current employees). Such vacancies pertain to high level jobs. This scope must be clear so no overlap between vacancies would happen.
3. **Recruitment Policy Approval Matrix:** this matrix identifies the stakeholders who should be involved in any recruitment process. For example, the authority to approve the hiring of a first level employee should be given to the HR and the department manager. The CEO shouldn't be involved in such decisions unless the company is a very small one and HR role is purely a strategic one which could necessitate the interference of a higher-level manager.
4. **Recruitment Procedure:** this section covers the following key areas:

- How the hiring request should begin and usually within this step the EFR (Employment Requisition Form) should be filled out as I explained previously in the work force requirements section.

- The expected time frame for the different recruitment stages, an example is illustrated in Figure 11.
- The roles and the expectations from all the stakeholders, line managers are required for example to exert the maximum effort to choose the best candidates according to the company's main guidelines.

5. **Appendix Section:** it includes all the required forms and documents that would support the stakeholders during the process, e.g. ERF, Reference Check Form, C&B (Compensation & Benefits) form, Candidate Evaluation Form...etc.

Figure 11 – Recruitment Cycle Time

Phase	Activities	Time Frame
1	Role identification, JD, and resume sourcing.	4 days
2	Initial HR screening / short-listing.	1 day
	Organising the Preliminary Interviews.	2 days
	Organising the Final Interviews.	2 days
	Debriefing sessions to take the final decisions.	1 day
4	Reference check.	2 days
3	Preparing the salary proposal, negotiate with the selected candidates and offer closure.	4 days

Again, the above elements are general and the composition of the recruitment policy could be longer or shorter as per the organisational conditions, its size, purpose and many other elements.

The Four Levels Measurement: Introduction

A lot of HR literature has been written on HR analytics and in some cases the writings of some authors were recognised as hallmarks. Of these writings is *The New HR Analytics* by Jac Fitz-Enz which goes deep into the HR analytics field through a research-based approach. Such writings are geared toward assisting HR professionals with advance experience.

For the purpose of this book and taking into consideration the level of the HR professionals that this book is targeting I will talk in a succinct way regarding the measurement topic for the HR functions covered within this model. Again, the measurement content in this book is reflecting my experience during a twelve-year period on what has made a difference in my performance and thus the HR organisational performance and so it's applicable only to the extent that the reader decides to be of benefit to his/her organisation.

The father of modern management Peter Drucker has once said, **"If you can't measure it you can't manage it."** The implementation of this principle has been a daunting challenge for HR professionals, researchers, academics and other HR practitioners who have been trying to quantify the contribution of the HR domain since decades ago.

The difficulty in quantifying the HR contribution and measuring the function's effectiveness stems out of many factors. Below are some of the most important ones:

1. The HR field is relatively new if we compared it with other well-established and matured functions like the finance and accounting not to mention that the birth of the strategic HR management was at mid-90s which means that before that the function was purely based on qualitative terms rather than quantitative ones. The journey to reach a high and mature level of the HR analytics requires a lot of effort and research in order to reach to the stage where the HR professionals all over the world are able to use a global HR analytics standard that is both globally accepted and locally customised.
2. The integration between the HR function and the other functions in the organisation is still weak. When it comes to the HR analytics HR people rely heavily on the input from the other departments to support their analytics dashboards. In this context integration means how much the other functions are well aware of the HR value to them and how they

understand that value to reflect it in their day-to-day people management issues. E.g. performance management analytics are not so effective if some department managers are making the most of their employees' evaluations around score 3 if we supposed that we have 5 scores rating scale. In such case the performance reviews analytics will reflect a pattern that most of the evaluations scores are around the central tendency. This means that the manager was reluctant to score the employee either low or high for hidden reasons (mostly to avoid the headache of justifying to the employee the rationale behind the low score or the fear of justifying the high scores for HR and senior management in order to support the performance evaluation decisions like giving the employee a salary raise).This weakness in the integration is distorting the HR analytics efforts even if the infrastructure for the analytics is robustly available. So, reaching to a high level of HR—Organisational integration is another obstacle to the HR analytics excellence.

3. HR field is based on many disciplines and the behavioural science of human beings is one of the most important disciplines. That's another obstacle in the face of the HR analytics. Human behaviour can't and will never be quantifiable. The outcomes of human beings in the workplace can't be measured by a yardstick, we ae not talking about the financial cash flow statement or the income statement and the analysis of the figures they contain, we are talking about people who react to different situations differently, and in some cases the same person could react differently to the same situation. This complexity makes the work of analytics even harder. Referring back to the example of performance management system analytics the issue of reaching valid analytics is disrupted by the subjectivity that accompanies the performance evaluation. Two managers could evaluate the same person with two different scores. As an example the relationship management competency standards as one of the evaluation criteria should lead in principle to similar evaluations from the two managers who are part of the 360-degree feedback tool to assess the HR manager's performance, but when it comes to take a decision on whether the HR manager is successful in building relationships with stakeholders, the outcome of the evaluation for the two managers differs by their perceptions. One of these managers could make a judgment on the HR manager based on a bad previous experience that she went through with the HR manager while the other could make positive evaluation. Unless the outcome of the two evaluations is scrutinised by talking with the two managers in more depth on the rationale behind their evaluations, the preliminary results are of no real value.

4. The most important factor in my opinion is the absence of standard HR model that is applicable to all organisations from all sizes and industries. This doesn't mean that a standard model is applicable completely in all the details even for two similar organisations. There should be always a

room for customisation. It's like the case in a P&L (Profit and loss) statement. The key elements are the same regardless of the organisation or the industry but the details could differ. The basic formula for the P&L statement is ((Revenue – cost of goods sold) – other expenses (e.g. operational)) the same but the difference lies in the elements of the operational expenses which is specific to the industry. In this book I am introducing a model that is gradual in its implementation and every stage builds upon on the previous one. If we reached to the point where the measurement framework (In this case the HR global model) is available then the measurement of that model would be easier and practical, as supposed that the HR analytics framework is also applicable worldwide as I mentioned in point number one.

The problems above reinforce the idea that HR analytics field is still based on ad-hoc basis. Which means that HR people create their own analytics framework as it's needed and a consistent measurement approach is not there yet. So, until we reach the optimal case of the HR analytics the HR function will suffer from the lack of appreciation and senior executives will still have the same critiques about the field. It's our role within this big uncertainty to revolutionise the function and how others are looking to it.

I will introduce the measurement side of this model as it pertains to every stage and by focusing on the most important metrics that would complement the model. This first topic to be covered under this category is recruitment, and the sequence that I will follow for the rest of this book is to introduce the model elements per each stage followed immediately by the measurement framework for each stage in order to have a complete loop.

Measuring Recruitment Effectiveness

Recruitment is considered as one of the most important basic functions of HR. Executives and business managers judge the success of the HR department within their companies of how much they are successful on their recruitment efforts. Business managers are always eager to achieve results and their measurement of any success is mostly linked with tangible outcomes. Recruitment outcomes are quantifiable to a large extent. When you go through a hiring procedure the expected outcome is to hire quickly and efficiently, these measures are manifested in the time you spend searching and hiring the needed talent and the performance results of the new comers during their early employment stages.

To tap into this area is a quick gain with regard to reaching an effective measurement framework, it's much easier to expand on a more quantifiable metrics like the time to hire than targeting more qualitative metrics like the company brand strength. In the first case the results are direct and more appealing to business executives who talk the numbers language while in the second case it's more difficult to attract the executives' attention on the engagement benchmark within the industry as related for example to the empowerment score (how much the employees are being given tools and resources to achieve their tasks). By following this approach, you begin the measurement framework on a small scale then you go bigger and stronger as you build on the accumulative experience that you get after every stage.

Within this topic I will introduce the following metrics:

1. Time to hire.
2. Cost per hire.
3. New hire retention percentage.
4. Cost of unfilled vacancies.
5. Recruitment yield ratios.

Time to Hire

The basic formula for this metric is so simple, it's based on taking the sum of days from when the vacancy was raised until it's closed by hiring the most qualified candidate as indicated by accepting the job offer. For example, if a vacancy was raised on 5th of June 2018 and the job offer was accepted on 20th of June then the time to hire in this case was 15 days.

Usually this metric is an indication on the recruitment function effectiveness on hiring on time or an indication on the delay to hire on time that might be caused by several reasons that I will talk about later on.

As mentioned before that this metric is very easy to calculate and to trace but the difficulty lies in improving the metric by decreasing the time needed to hire someone. A one-size-fits-all approach is not effective anymore when it comes to recruitment and more specifically to sourcing candidates. Recruitment goes into a sequence of the following stages as depicted in Figure 12.

Figure 12 – Recruitment Stages

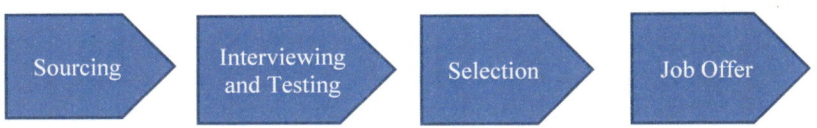

The first stage is very critical in order to guarantee the continuity to the other stages. Most of the recruitment activities fall short because the source of their hires is either not generating enough candidates or because the source in itself is not generating highly qualified candidates. The issue of identifying the most suitable and effective recruitment source is not a scientific formula that you follow through all the times and in all the situations. It's a matter of trial and error approach.

I recall very much how easy it was 12 years ago to find candidates through one or two recruitment channels at most. At that time most of the candidates whom I found were generated through the newspaper's ads. But the world since that time has changed a lot. The advent of social media as a breakthrough has opened a new era for the whole world. HR function was affected in a dramatic way by social media, branding as an example doesn't need to be all physical. You don't have to participate in all the job fairs in your town in order to promote for the employment benefits you offer, social media can guarantee for you an effective presence and high visibility for millions of people with little effort.

Recruitment has also been affected positively by social media, it's much easier to locate candidates through social media platforms than to search for them through other channels like job boards. In order to be more effective in your recruitment you need to identify the most suitable source per every job family you have in your organisations and in some cases, you will need to identify the source per each job within certain job families. Source identification does not happen overnight. Through my tenure as an HR manager for a heavy equipment company I spent a couple of years searching for the best recruitment source in order to find qualified service operations managers.

As most HR professionals do when initiating a new vacancy, I begun the search through the local channels I have within my country. I spent months searching for the service operations manager whether through local job boards, local head-hunters, local specialised weekly newspapers and many more but the result was disappointing. I expanded my search circle to outside the country by seeking regional job boards and head-hunters. It took me several months also until I found a major and well-known job board in the gulf region. It had a big expansion in the gulf area for many heavy equipment companies which eventually helped me to find qualified candidates that made my search easier.

In other cases where I was searching for highly specialised mining technicians, I had to go to specialised mining job boards in order to find the suitable candidates. So, it must be clear now that as a professional recruiter you need to realise that recruitment sourcing is maximised when you are able to gear your sourcing to the right channel which in turn will save you time and thus decreasing the time to hire.

It's worth mentioning that in some cases you can't hire just by going externally to locate candidates, you need to look internally if this is the case. When I was preparing the workforce plan for the mining section it was required to hire 30 technicians locally. Through a one-year time frame we interviewed and tested almost 300 hundred candidates, which means that we chose one technician from every ten candidates. Such rate was alarming and it was a confirmation on the weakness of the vocational training centres in Jordan. In order to overcome this problem in case a future booming happened again we decided to design an accelerated apprenticeship program that prepares technical diploma graduates (two years degree) within a one-year time frame for the level one technician job role which would serve any new mining project.

So, it's important to realise that decreasing the time to hire requires two things:

1. To exert a diligent research on the best external talent sources per each job family or position.
2. To build internal talent pipeline for critical jobs that are extremely difficult to be filled externally like the apprenticeship programs.

But now comes also the key question, how can we enhance the sourcing channels in order to maintain these channels effective in generating qualified candidates? There are a lot of tools and techniques you can use. Below are some of the most important ones I have found to be very valuable in supporting your sourcing strategy:

1. Defining a talent acquisition strategy beforehand, most of the problems occur when the talent acquisition is being tackled on a demand-basis approach, which means that HR begins the search for the candidates once a requisition order has been initiated by the line managers. Even if you have a robust network of recruitment sources your effectiveness won't be at its best if you don't know about a hiring need in advance, the time you take to understand the business needs behind the requisition, the time to study any alternative solution other than hiring new employees and the efforts to prepare for and organise the search process all are counted against your time to hire target. You need to work with your managers in a participative approach through the workforce strategy design stage (I highlighted in that issue in the HR-Organisation strategy alignment topic) in order to understand their workforce needs and to be equipped with all the info you need in order to maximise your search and thus enhancing the time needed to hire someone.
2. Recruitment technology integration with your recruitment strategy, applicant tracking systems are very important to your time to hire metric especially if recruitment comprises a big bulk of your HR operational activities. The time you usually take to organise the internal recruitment process (the flow of the hiring process between HR and line managers) are a big headache for even the most seasoned recruiters. ATS helps to automate the huge paper work that accompanies any recruitment process (this area was discussed in the Recruitment and Technology topic) and thus saving you valuable time that you can take advantage of for other strategic recruitment issues.
3. You need to be creative in finding new recruitment sources. As we said before that the world is changing rapidly and so people all around the globe are also changing their habits in order to keep with that changing pace. I remember how I established a network with the local maintenance garages in my town in order to expand the service technicians' pipeline. It was unusual practice at that time for a prestigious heavy equipment company to follow that approach but it paid dividends that outpaced the efforts we exerted. Candidates who are illiterate with technology usage will be shortly highly professional users

of that technology like the smart phone's technology. The number of people who are using smart phones is increasing rapidly which will open the door for the mobile apps-based career pages as a new recruitment source. You need to be vigilant in your sourcing strategy if you want to keep your time to hire metric competitive.
4. Keep the channels with the targeted candidates open and thriving. Creating a talent pool that is both abundant and quality-based would support your sourcing strategy for the long run.
5. The aforementioned factors won't negate the importance of the traditional marketing tools and techniques like participating in job fairs, promoting for your employment benefits on social media, participating in community service events and so on.

The last point I want to discuss here is the implications of time to hire metric on both recruitment cost and quality of the candidates.

* When you are hiring you need to keep eye on the cost factor. Some recruiters would speed the recruitment cycle by contacting the most well-known head-hunters in order to find their desired candidate quickly. This would be okay if the cost associated with the process is affordable and rational to incur. Others would take their time to hire the desired candidate regardless of the time boundaries, their major goal is to save cost. Nothing is wrong with that approach as long as the cost of the unfilled vacancy and the lost opportunity calculations are being considered.
* The second factor that you need to examine carefully is quality of the hire. If you speed the process of hiring because you are being faced with big pressure from your management then the quality of the hire could be compromised, on the other side if you take your time to hire in order to find highly qualified candidates then you might find the talent you wish to have but the cost of the unfilled vacancy and the lost opportunity factors are going to be high which will impact the economic well-being of your corporation.

The time to hire metric is very crucial metric to make sure that you are being efficient in your recruitment activities and it's very easy also to trace it but the difficulty lies on tackling the details of that metric and how to mitigate its risk. Following through the above factors would be of great value for you in order to be able to capture the benefits of tracking that metric and reflecting it on the overall company's performance.

Cost Per Hire

The main goal behind that metric is to know what's the average cost of hiring a person into your organisation. It's based on taking the sum of the internal and external cost divided by the number of hires within a certain time period.

This metric is very important for budgetary purposes as it serves the HR department in allocating the hiring cost correctly and efficiently. It's also helpful in making a standard cost level for the job categories in your organisation which enables you to find ways to cut these costs as applicable and without compromising the quality of hire.

As for the previous metric (Time to Hire) this one is also easy to be tracked but the there is some hardship in gathering the needed data to calculate the metric.

Usually this metric is calculated following two methods:

1. The first method is to calculate the metric internally within the organisational boundaries without making a comparison with any other organisation. The formula to calculate this metric is highlighted below. The cost elements for this metric are specific to the organisation.

$$\text{Cost per Hire} = \frac{\text{External cost} + \text{internal cost}}{\text{Number of hires in a time period}}$$

In the table below you will find a sample element of the Internal and External Costs.

Internal Costs	External Costs
Recruiting team training expenses.	Medical check fees.
Recruiting team compensation cost.	Travel expenses for candidates.
Line managers' cost (who participate in the process).	Job fair fees.
	Head-hunter fees.

2. The second method is to calculate this metric externally by comparing the cost of hire for the organisation with other organisations within the same or similar industries. The goal is to have a continuous benchmark in order to decrease the cost according to the acceptable cost levels of other organisations. The formula to calculate this metric is the same as for the previous one but the cost is restricted to specific elements that are shared between the organisations that benchmark against each other.

The shift from the first method through the second bears another difficulty in gathering the needed information. In the first case you have the ultimate control on the data as it's already at your fingertips while in the other you need to exert more effort to gather the data from multiple sources and it also needs coordination and organising skills to gather the needed data correctly.

You can notice that as we move from one metric to another the information gathering process becomes harder, it's much more easy to gather information related to the time to hire than to gather information for the cost per hire metric but the value that the organisation might capture is higher in the cost per hire metric. Here the time it took you to bring someone onboard is translated into monetary terms which gives more meaning to your senior managers when examining such metrics.

New Hire Retention Percentage

Through this metric you can know the percentage of the employees who stayed in the organisation after the probation period. It's calculated by dividing the number of separations during the probation period by the average headcount for the same period as indicated by the following formula.

100 − (Separations during probation period / Average headcount × 100)

This metric is very important for you to measure your hiring efforts' success. There are many other factors that would contribute to the separation of the new hires even if your hiring procedure was effective. For example, if the onboarding system is not effective in supporting these new hires which would affect the retention percentage negatively. But within this context we are relating this metric to the recruitment process' effectiveness.

This metric is very easy to track also and the information you need to calculate it is also easy to gather but it has less value to the organisational leaders as it's not reflected into financial terms.

Cost of Unfilled Vacancies

This metric is considered one of the most difficult metrics to track and measure because to identify (as we will see in the formula) the lost revenue for a vacant position is very difficult. It could be possible to identify the lost revenue for sales positions although in this case the estimation is not completely accurate but the difficult part of this metric is when you have managerial and administrative positions that are not revenue generation positions.

Because of the difficulty to gather indicative information this metric is the least to be used within the above-mentioned metrics although the value of such metric to the organisational executives is very high. It's even the highest in terms of the value consideration amongst the above metrics because it highlights financially what are the losses of having certain positions open and unfilled.

This metric is a double-edged sword, if the opportunity cost behind certain positions is very high then the first party to be blamed for this is you (the HR person) unless the reasons for the unfilled vacancy is beyond your control, let's say that the warehouse manager decided few months ago that hiring a warehouse inventory coordinator is not a priority. It's your role here to show the cost of this unfilled vacancy and the impact it has on business. On the other side showing the data behind this metric would help to reveal the importance of the vacant position to the overall organisational health or it could show that this vacancy has no major effect on the organisation, which would support future workforce planning decisions. The decision could be not to increase the headcount in certain positions which could lead to direct savings in the headcount budget and an increased efficiency with the remaining headcount.

The formula of this metric is the following:

(Average revenue per employee per day × number of days position was open) + cost of alternative solutions (overtime, temporary workers) − (average compensation per employee per day × number of days position was open).

Recruitment Yield Ratios

This segment of the recruitment metrics is about studying the details of every recruitment stage to determine the effectiveness of each stage in delivering the required talent in terms of the quantity and the quality. In order to understand these ratios better let's first envision how a traditional recruitment process looks like. Figure 13 (Recruitment Funnel) lists the recruitment stages that are applicable in most organisations.

Figure 13 – Recruitment Funnel

Let's now analyse every stage in terms of the recruitment yield ratios and how these stages could be better maximized to their greatest yield.

- At the first stage (Organisational Brand) which will be discussed later on in this book all what we care about is to create a true and compelling image of our organisation that plays a key role in attracting the needed talent in order to build the talent pipeline. Examining this stage's yield capability enables us to identify the best course of action that we must follow in order to have an effective brand strategy. An example would be looking at the number of resumes you get when participating in a job fair. This is the simplest way you look at your brand efforts yield capability. A more strategic metric to look at is the engagement level of your organisation as a brand indication (this issue will be discussed later on). If the number of resumes you got after you have participated in the job fair wasn't as desired then you must examine if this job fair was the right one to participate in or you could examine if the HR personnel who represented your company were qualified in promoting your EVP (Employees Value Proposition).
- Sourcing is the second stage in the recruitment funnel, we talked about this stage comprehensively in the time to hire metric. Again, what you need to do in order to examine the yield ratio of this stage is to look at the number of successful hires yielded from every source. If LinkedIn is generating highly qualified IT professionals then you should use this source whenever you have a vacancy in the IT department. But you should consider your marketplace and its competitiveness continuously as today's workforce is not predictable anymore. The IT professionals you found on LinkedIn would still have their profiles on LinkedIn but they could move to specialised IT recruitment agencies if the jobs they get would pay them high compensation. The effectiveness of your recruitment source is how dynamic and effective it is in generating highly qualified candidates in the shortest time possible. Going to LinkedIn in that case doesn't mean that you will find what you are searching for.
- Screening is the stage through which you go quickly through the resumes you got and you match their suitability with the job requirements. During this stage the recruiters would make quick phone interviews for further investigation. The yield ratio deficiency within this stage is attributed to many factors; one of these factors could be the screening criteria which could be lofty and would unintentionally eliminate good resumes.
- The blockers at the interviewing stage is mostly caused by unqualified interviewers and in this case the interviewer could be the line manager and mostly these managers focus on the technical competencies for the candidates which would result in hiring candidates who are culturally unfit. The other problem could be the interview errors that most of the recruiters make. The HR person who is making the interview could judge the candidate based on a key strength that she discovered in the interview (e.g. the candidate is strong in the analytical reasoning) and

subsequently gives their approval on hiring the candidate despite their weakness in many other areas that the recruiter failed to explore.
- At the assessment stage the most important thing is to examine your testing procedure against its job performance predictability. In other words, if a candidate passed with a high score the sales skills situational assessment then it's expected that the actual performance for the candidate on the job is distinguished with high performance. Otherwise there is a problem with the test validation which requires you to review if the test is the right one to use.
- Most of the problems that companies struggle with when it comes to offering the job to a candidate is the risk of the counter offers that the candidate's current employer would submit. These risks decrease the yield ratio of your job offers' stage. Here you need to discover if the candidate is really interested in your company during the interview stage by focusing on the cultural fit area that is most probably overlooked. You could expect for example that the candidate will accept your job offer if the compensation you offered is slightly higher than the candidate's current package but despite of that she has expressed her interest to work with your company. Such indicators would encourage you to submit job offers that most probably are going to be accepted rather than wasting your time on giving offers that the candidate will reject.

If you reached the hiring stage successfully then you have a recruitment process with an acceptable yielding capability. This comes after your onboarding process and how effective it is in retaining your best talent. This yield ratio analysis is expressed in many formulas as stated below (these ratios are just an example):

Qualified Applicant	Applicants Passed Test	Offers Accepted
Total Applicants	Total Applicants	Offers Submitted

A key question should be introduced here; is this analysis applicable all the times? Answering this question depends on one major factor. It's the organisation's size. This factor reflects on the recruitment activities which will determine if this analysis should be done frequently or not. Big organisations that recruit big numbers annually gain a lot of benefits when doing such analysis.

The saving in time and efforts form one stage to another when you have a big recruitment department with large number of recruiters that has a large financial effect on the company, not to mention the efficiency gained from saving time and money as related to scale advantage. Mid-sized and small companies won't necessarily have the reason to do this analysis unless there is a need to do so. This means that when the HR department is facing a yield problem in certain recruitment stages then they can do such analysis covering a timeframe in order to capture the problems in the yield capability. Let's say that the test has been classified as not valid for certain job roles which resulted in fewer number of applicants.

Once the problem is resolved then you don't have to do this analysis continuously as there is no use in excreting this analysis if the number of recruits doesn't justify the cause of doing the analysis. In order to capture this analysis correctly when you have a small organisation you need to have a robust recruitment data base that you can get back to when you have a need.

Before ending this subject, I want to emphasise on the importance of realising the benefits you could reap from choosing the best fit metrics for your industry and specifically your organisation. The metrics I included within this book were fine and suitable for my needs at certain period. You should definitely choose what is best for you and most importantly to measure what should be measured, don't try to measure everything.

This will lead you to what we call the analysis paralysis. HR analytics is the differentiator the sets you apart from your peers so take advantage of it and focus on what should be measured in order to be accomplished.

In order to make your life easier when it comes to choosing the best HR metrics for your organisation, I have made a comparison between the aforementioned recruitment metrics as an illustration for you to build upon when choosing the best fit metrics for your organisation.

This illustration summarises the tracking potential of every metric in terms of the frequency of using the metric. It also clarifies how much the information availability affects the metrics choice and determining the value of using the metric to your organisation in terms of how much these recruitment metrics could be quantified as a cost factor that shows how much the organisation is spending on recruitment and how much is the cost that the organisation incurs because of not hiring the needed talent on time. This illustration is listed below in Figure 14 (Recruitment Metrics Comparison).

Figure 14 – Recruitment Metrics Value Comparison

	Tracking Potential	Information Availability	Value to the Org. (Cost Factor)
Time to Hire	High	High	Low
New Hire Retention			
Cost of Unfilled Vacancy			
	Low	Low	High

Following the above graph would help you to conceptualise which metric to pursue first according to the easiness of applying the metrics directly and how much information is available. In our case it's much more rational to begin with time to hire and new hire retention rate and once the metrics are applied and the value of the information behind the metrics is captured, we can move forward to the rest of the metrics.

Building analytics competency becomes easier if you begin small then you gradually widen the scale of the implementation building on accumulated reservoir of HR metrics understanding after each stage.

Total Rewards

Introduction

Now we will move to the next element in the second part of the foundational HR (Level One), it's the total rewards which comes under the service delivery category.

Employees have gone far away in their expectations regarding the compensation and the benefits they aspire to have. Historically in the past employees were more satisfied than today and this is evident in the engagement scores on a world-wide scale. Employees were happy if they were working in a stable work environment, they were more interested in an employer who cared about them. This is not to lessen the effect of the direct side of the rewards they get. Here we talk about the net cash regardless of what the cash elements are. They cared about the cash, but not to the degree that it would shadow the other intangible elements.

Nowadays the paradigm has shifted a lot. Now the employees are more demanding, they want hire basic salaries, they want more advancement opportunities than before. There is nothing wrong with that; isn't it the principle that the modern organisations have been established upon. To provide the best and the most alluring work experience so that the employee is attached to the organisation deeply and continuously, yes it is! And total rewards are a key element in this principle, but the challenge is how to make the needed balance between offering the appropriate mix of the total rewards that would attract talent and retain the current employees in addition to maintaining an excellent bottom line organisational result.

There are many reasons for that shift, the globalisation had the biggest effect on almost all the HR functions and total rewards were affected dramatically to the degree that the composition of any total reward system for any employee is not the same anymore. This change happened relatively in a short period. I remember clearly how the health insurance coverage was considered a key and competitive element in my total reward package 12 years ago, and it was an element that I used heavily in the TR negotiation phase with any candidate. It paid dividends at that time. For the time being I forget in many interviews to mention it and the candidates in most of these cases don't ask about it. It has become a built-in feature within the TR system. You can't use it any more as a competitive-edge.

This openness to the modern world (Globalisation) has made the awareness level for the employee in any organisation very high. Employees are no longer in need to wait their employer to tell them at the yearend ceremony what has happened in their industry in terms of the competitive landscape and its effect on the total rewards that the industry is offering. Social media and the instant connection it brings has alleviated the complexity of the old communication model. Employees don't have to search for information any more. Subscribing to a mobile application like Glassdoor would give you a big advantage on exploring what the competition is paying to its employees.

Transparency is now a key driver in the employer-employee relationship. This aspect is a success factor in any HR issue you could ever face as an HR professional. Total rewards mostly are noticed as the most factor that could be affected by a transparent communication policy. In principle it is, in terms of the direct effect it has on employee morale. Employers would gain many benefits if they for example published on their intranet the salaries of the employees so everyone would know how much others are being paid. TR is the segment that is mostly desirable and wanted from all the employees. But TR transparency effect starts very big at the beginning and then gets smaller by time in favour of more strategic HR functions like the performance management. This relationship is illustrated in Figure 15 as a comparison between TR and performance management. This relationship is reciprocal for all the other HR functions.

Figure 15 – HR Transparency Effect Graph

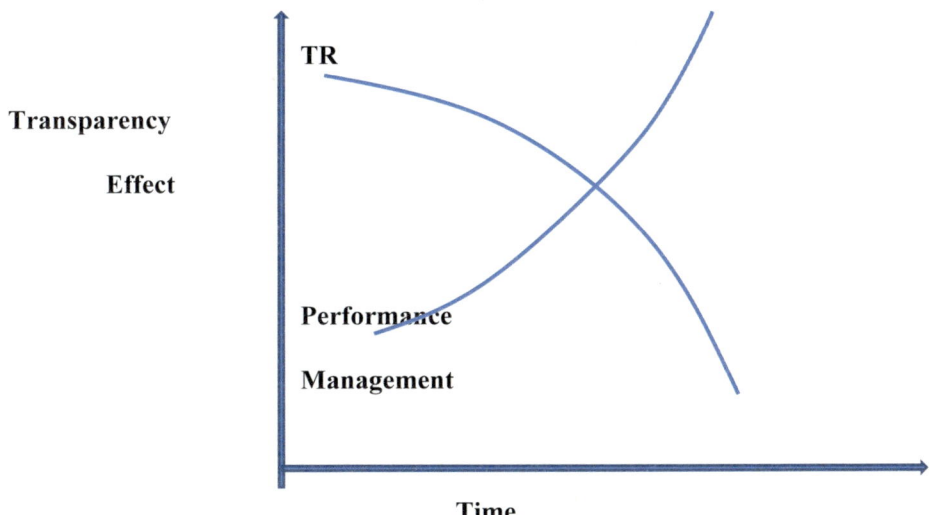

Another aspect of the globalisation is the rapid increase of the virtual workplace, we hear a lot about many organisations that have no physical presence at all. Such organisations might have a global network of diverse employees in terms of their locations, backgrounds, their origin…etc. and they do their tasks remotely with no direct communication with each other.

Such technological breakthrough increases the competitiveness as employees all over the world are now more inclined to such work arrangement which will enable them to spare time for their families and thus enhancing their well-being. The most important advantage that the employee gain from this type of work is the compensation that they get. It's usually higher than the other traditional go-to-work arrangements. The rationale behind giving high compensation for these people is that they are required to have high communication and project management skills so they would be able to deal with the complexity that such work brings. This issue has increased the burden that employers are now required to offer competitive total rewards in order to retain their employees to keep the motivation high for them. Some would argue that the future of work is going to be virtual and I believe so but that wouldn't negate the importance of the physical workplace as a major factor in the business relations that constitute the corner stone of any workplace, and so comes the controversial question, when this virtual workplace is going to dominate?

The above factors are just two examples of the implications that the globalisation brings over and their effects on total rewards systems. The effects of globalisation are endless.

It's worth mentioning as we talk about globalisation that there are other factors that affect the total rewards system deeply. Here I am talking about political instability as a Factor that might affect the total rewards system. A concrete example is the Arab spring that happened in the Arab region few years ago, and its impact on total rewards.

The nature of the Arab culture and the impact it generated in terms of the paternalistic way of governing every single aspect of Arab daily life has made the trend going for many years around a transactional total reward system. As a reflected on the business sector this means that the business leaders and managers were used to a more direct rewards approach that uses monetary bonuses and prizes to recognise good performers while using on the other side traditional punishment methods to adjust or correct bad performance.

This prevailing trend that lasted for decades has prevented the healthy employee-employer dialogue as a prerequisite for a successful and thriving mutual relationship. Employees were reluctant to demand for better business conditions. Unfair business practices were accepted as a normal practice and most importantly employees were always searching for the intrinsic side of the motivation that meant a lot for them. All these factors have contributed to a high level of frustration for the youth who comprises a big portion of the workforce in the Arab world.

Arab spring has changed the whole picture. Here I will not go into the details of that game changer event. The vital issue here is the impact that this event has brought, and it was to a big extent very positive impact if we eliminated the catastrophic conditions that hit some countries. In countries where they dealt with that turmoil in a more peaceful way the effect was really amazing, Jordan is a key example here. Citizens are now more open and more relieved talking about political issues that were prohibited before.

Employees also are now more encouraged to demand for better working conditions, better compensation. They have more autonomy to choose the elements of the total rewards that they believe would constitute a value for them. Things have changed now and the pace of change is accelerating to the degree that employers are under the big pressure of leveraging the modern workplace as non-negotiable fact and providing a competitive total reward is not an exception, gone are the days when total rewards were administered separately as a non-strategic part of the total employee experience.

What I have just mentioned is a clarification on how HR is being affected by the external surroundings and in turn affecting the internal environment (the workplace). HR responds by being a proactive business partner whether it was a total reward system or any other HR system.

Being proactive when it comes to total rewards requires a diligent market research on the latest market trends on the best and most competitive total rewards offerings in the marketplace and taking corrective action if needed to have an organisational total reward strategy that is internally equitable and externally competitive, this area will be examined also in more depth in subsequent sections.

Before we examine the areas of total reward in more detail, let's define total rewards first. Total rewards include all the financial and non-financial elements that the employee perceives of having a real value whether it was a remuneration (basic pay, bonuses, commissions, overtime pay…etc.) or benefits (health insurance coverage, retirement benefit…etc.).

Most commonly this definition is widely recognised and accepted between the HR professionals. But here lies the problem, accepting this definition as final would really put us in front of many problems when it comes to employees' motivation. But what's the definition of motivation. The word is originated from the Latin word *mover* which means "to move." The essence of motivation is to make the employee want to make something which is in this regard to do his/her tasks efficiently and to contribute in achieving the organisational goals.

How can we motivate the employee to excel at his/her work and to keep that motivation high and continuous? Depending only on the financial and non-financial elements to motivate the employee won't be enough. You can give your employees the highest compensation possible within your industry as part of your retention strategy in order to keep the best employees but to find at the end of the year that the engagement results are not up to the required standards and that your financial returns are also below the industry acceptable revenue standards.

A CEO would ask, how that could be although the competition is paying far below us? Here comes your role as an HR practitioner to highlight on the hidden areas that most companies don't focus on. It's the intrinsic side of motivation that is far away from the definition we just previewed. Within this area you need to make it clear for every manager you have in your organisation that motivating employees by understanding their needs and the trigger behind their actions is complementary part to the traditional total rewards concept.

Employees everywhere are more inclined to a work environment that has a culture of open communication that would really make the difference in their daily work life. We are dealing with human beings who have different needs and personalities. HR professionals must educate and train the managers on how to understand these different personalities and accordingly to steer their actions in a customised way that fits every employee. As a fact no two employees are the same. There is the type of employees who are motivated by being part of something bigger, they are more attracted to teamwork, they are naturally more productive when they work with teammates they like. Such employees must be included as much as possible in project-based tasks in order to bring the best out of them.

There is also another type of employees who are motivated when they are exposed to challenging tasks that are appealing to their personal preferences. Such employees must be given over and over new and challenging tasks and most importantly to give them the full control on the task execution. By that you can guarantee that the motivation level for your employee is energized to serve their inside triggers and to achieve the organisational goals in the best possible way.

In summary, total rewards should be monitored by HR professionals as a balanced approach between intrinsic and extrinsic motivators that if combined with each other successfully then the result would be a tremendous momentum that will add on the organisational horse power in moving the organisation to the optimal competitive position.

Total Rewards Essentials

Total Rewards System Design

We mentioned before that TR (Total Rewards) is a key driver to motivate the workforce of any organisation, of course if taken by its both sides, the intrinsic and the extrinsic. Unfortunately, most the employers are afraid of tackling the problems behind their TR systems.

They mostly link any adjustment or enhancement in their TR systems with having to incur high costs and/or benefits restructuring that mostly don't yield any noticeable returns. This problem is widely affecting the engagement level of the employees. The biggest effect is the resulting demotivation of the employees and the harm it brings to the organisation in terms of the lost productivity and the high turnover rate.

HR has an important role here. A robust approach that HR should use is to identify from the beginning of the TR system design what is the purpose of the system. This should be done before we identify our TR strategy which is based on three major areas:

1. The first one is to match the market. Here the organisation TR elements are similar to what the competition is introducing.
2. The second one is to lead the market. Here the organisation offers more competitive TR packages than the competition.
3. The last one is to lag the market. Here the organisation's TR packages are less competitive than the prevailing packages in the marketplace and the industry.

The above three strategies are determinant of the course of action that the organisation will follow in terms of the pay structure design, employment benefits scope and other elements that complement the TR system. But they don't help to achieve the organisational goals unless they are linked with the main purpose of the TR system.

When we talk about the purpose of the total reward system, we should put into consideration that this purpose must be a reflection of the organisational purpose (Mission).

Let's suppose that your organisation's mission is the following, **we serve our customers everywhere on the highest standards in the industry by offering unique and reliable products that make their life easier.** Such purpose bears a lot of interactions that have many reflections on many organisational disciplines including the total rewards strategy as our topic of discussion.

In such case the organisation is searching for excellence (serving our customers on the highest standards) which means that competitiveness should be a major driver of your total reward system. Having for example front-end customer service centre requires a type of workforce who possesses high relationship building skills and high customer orientation. Such workforce can't be attracted easily unless you have high compensation.

Another important factor that must be included within your total reward package in order to accomplish your main organisational purpose is the development opportunities the company is offering to its workforce. The motivation of the workforce won't be complete unless you supplement your TR package with training and development opportunities.

In order to complete the loop as related to our previous example we should formulate the following TR mission (Philosophy) statement that reflects the previous elements. We can say the following, "We offer our employees competitive compensation and benefits that instils the sense of partnership in the organisation's overall interest and in turn we expect from them to treat their customers with the highest customer service standards."

Such TR statement is reflective of the organisational statement and thus the synergy between the formulation of the TR statement and its implementation is going to be high, in other words the HR will be in a better place to see a real connection between what the organisation is offering and what's really happening on the ground.

By following this approach HR manager would be able to justify the investments that the organisation should pursue as result of their TR benchmark with the market. In this context HR must define the measurement framework for the success of the TR system. In our example the HR manager can design an opinion survey that elicits the showrooms' managers' opinions about whether the compensation system is driving the performance of the showroom customer service representatives.

The survey could ask the following questions, on a scale of 1 to 4 how did the commission scheme for the customer service reps has contributed to new customers and revenue generation? Another question would be, on a scale of 1 to 4 how the development plans of the customer service reps is driving the organisational mission? Such questions and other similar ones would help you to identify if the TR elements are driving the performance of the employees and thus the organisational performance which will be the basis for the next step.

The next step after we have identified the TR mission statement is to match our compensation system with the previous three pay strategies (Match, Lead and Lag). Then we begin the design of the benefits packages in order to complete the loop of having effective C&B (Compensation and benefits) structure.

Compensation System Design

Compensation are the financial elements that are paid to the employees beyond the available benefits packages. I mentioned in the introduction that the effect of this side on the overall employee experience is very high at the beginning. The main driver for the employee when they join the organisation is the TR package but even if that package was luring enough to attract the candidates to the organisation this effect begins to fade away once the employee is settled down in the organisation. The employee becomes more concerned about other vital issues like building relationships with colleagues and managers.

But still the thoughtful design and execution of an attractive C&B packages is still a make or break factor that open the door for other key strategic areas. The employee won't be very much satisfied within her employment just because she has a visionary manager and supportive colleagues. The C&B package must be excellent enough so the employee won't be dragged emotionally every time she thinks of her C&B package and how unfair it is compared with her colleagues'. It's like a trainer who is a subject matter expert in his field but his motivation capabilities are not equivalent to his knowledge. The trainees would go out of the training session equipped with the needed skills but their overall satisfaction from the training experience wasn't high.

The compensation system design goes through the following stages.

Figure 16 – Compensation System Design

Job Analysis and Job Description → Job Evaluation → Pay Structure Design

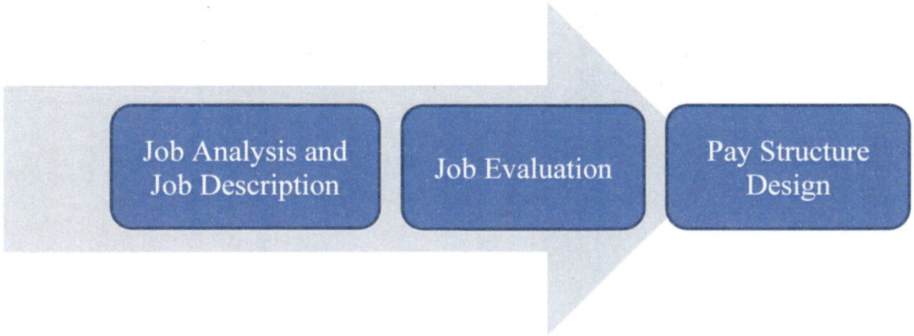

Again, and as a key principle that this book was built upon, I will not go into the details of the first phase (Job Description and Job Analysis) although they are very important and any mistakes done during this phase will have its negative effects on the rest of the other phases. The main reason for that is the abundance of information available on the topic in addition to the easiness of implementation. For the purpose of this book job evaluation is going to be discussed in details because it's a less discussed HR topic due to several reasons. The system is complex and its complexity is derived from the wide scope of stakeholders (managers and employees) who must be included in the system design and implementation with a high interference at both the design and the implementation phases. The system is also based on a trial and error approach when it comes to implementation which adds to the overall complexity of the system. Job analysis and description processes on the other hand are mainly controlled and executed to a high degree through the HR person with a high degree of stakeholders (managers and employees) intervention at the design phase and a little interference at other stages of job documentation (Job description) and distribution to the organisation.

Job Evaluation

Now let's define the job evaluation process. It's the process through which you identify the relative worth (Value) of a job within an organisation with other jobs in order to establish a structure that shows the order of jobs for the purpose of establishing an equitable grade structure.

Job evaluation is about valuing the job, not the person. This is a major principle that all of your job evaluation schemes must be built upon. You should expect to a great extent that when introducing the job evaluation for the first time into your organisation that most of the stakeholders whom you work with to apply this methodology will have a confusion at first between the job and the person. You will hear them saying over and over "who is much more valuable to the organisation, John or Emma."

Here comes your role as an advisor to your organisation and to make it clear that the main purpose of this methodology is to weigh the importance of the job, not the person. This overlap would make the organisation fall into the trap of valuing the person rather than the job and thus favouring one job over another by relying on a purely subjective judgment. Of course, such a mistake is more obvious and applicable to the non-quantitative job evaluation schemes (e.g. job ranking) that I will talk about briefly in this section. In a quantitative-based job evaluation the severity of that error is less affecting but it could make the process slower than should be as you are obliged to clear this misunderstanding every time you face it from the stakeholders who are involved in the process.

Job evaluation has many benefits:

1. It enables the HR department to establish for a valid case when it comes to job allocation decisions based on a systematic criterion. HR can assign a certain job for a person based on the job evaluation factors that determines if a person is eligible to undertake the job or not. It's much more easier to assign a supervisory role for a high potential employee based on a clear criterion like the decision-making scope (in this case the new supervisor is required to make independent judgment within the scope of her department otherwise she must request the guidance of her superior) than just to assign the job haphazardly with no clear guidance.
2. Job evaluation is the first step toward establishing the pay structure that is both internally equitable and externally competitive. Pay decisions based on job evaluation necessitates that the organisation must benchmark their basic pay with what's being offered in the industry and thus the competition in order to have an integrated grade and pay structure.

3. Based on the outcome of the job evaluation process (the grade and the pay structure) the organisation would be in a stronger position to make rational and defensible decisions regarding the career transitions from one grade to another because the hierarchy of jobs in the grade structure follows a systematic way of justifying why one job had a higher rank than the other which would eliminate the confusion regarding the unrealistic expectations of an employee to go two or more steps in the grade structure. Also, the transition within the pay range for a given grade would be much more defensible for the organisation because the grade structure should be complimented with a systematic pay ranges that take into account a realistic pay boundary that make it easy to make fair pay decisions.
4. When you have effective and competitive grade and pay structures then you can use it as an attraction tool into your recruitment strategy. Candidates are more inclined to companies that secure guaranteed pay and career progression.
5. The existence as we mentioned before of an equitable and defensible grade and pay structures is one of the levers in creating an engagement culture. Employees would be more engaged and they would trust the organisational leadership when their career progression and pay decisions are being made and displayed transparently.

Job Evaluation Types

Job evaluation has two types, the first one is the quantitative (Analytical) job evaluation which assigns a score to the jobs being evaluated through a reference to a scaling system that is applicable to all the jobs. Within this type of job evaluation, the weight of the personal judgment in the evaluation process is very low, here the advantage is in the high objectivity that accompanies such schemes. The two well-known methods of this scheme are the Factor Comparison and the Point-Factor Scheme.

The second type of job evaluation is the Non-Quantitative (Non-Analytical) Job Evaluation which establishes a hierarchy (Order) of jobs as compared with each other. The degree of subjectivity (Personal judgment) in this type of job evaluation is very high. The two well-known methods of this scheme are the Job Ranking and the Job Classification.

There is an overlap between these two schemes as related to the following criteria:

- The job-to-job comparison.
- The job-to-predetermined-standard comparison.

This overlap is represented in the following table (Job Evaluation Types):

Job Evaluation Types

Comparison Criteria	Non-Quantitative Schemes	Quantitative Schemes
Job-to-Job Comparison	Job Ranking	Factor Comparison
Job-to-Predetermined-Standard Comparison	Job Classification	Point-Factor scheme

Job ranking and job classification are being considered non-quantitative job evaluation methods but the job ranking method is considered as a job-to-job comparison while the job classification is considered as a job-to-predetermined-standard comparison. Job classification has more objectivity than the job ranking.

On the other hand, the factor comparison and the point-factor methods are being considered quantitative job evaluation methods but factor comparison is a job-to-job comparison like the job ranking while the point-factor scheme is a job-to-predetermined-standard comparison like the job classification.

In a job-to-job comparison the difference between job ranking and factor comparison lies in the scoring scale that is assigned to the factor comparison method which gives a dollar value for every job in the scoring matrix. In a job-to-predetermined-standard comparison the difference between job classification and point-factor method lies in the standard against which these two schemes are being compared to. The standard in the job classification is categorised in segments that details a description of every segment while the standard in the point-factor method is the scoring scale.

Historically job ranking was the most common job evaluation method, the problem with it as we stated earlier is the high subjectivity in making evaluation judgment in addition to falling into the mistake of overlapping between the person and the job. Other job evaluation methods like the factor comparison and the job classification methods were developed to add more rationality to the evaluation process but still the subjectivity issue was a concern although it was less obvious than in the job ranking method.

In the 1950s Hay group developed the point job evaluation method that analyses the job into factors through which the job is being valued (the size of the job is determined). This methodology was the basis from which most of the point-factor schemes were originated. The point factor method is the most reliable job evaluation method because of its high validity and objectivity in making the judgement. But still we must be alerted to the fact that all the job evaluation methods hold a degree of subjectivity including the point-factor method. The advantage in choosing one method over the other is how much is one method is more objective than the other. This comparison between the job evaluation methods and how they relate to each other will be highlighted in Figure 16 (Job Evaluation Methods Comparison).

But before that let's summarise briefly the following three types of the job evaluation methods before we go into more details of the point-factor method:

- Job Ranking: is the method of comparing one job to another within an organisation in order to establish a hierarchy of jobs from highest to lowest in terms of their value to the organisation.
- Job Classification: is the process of establishing a number of grades or classes, each having its definition or description and accordingly to slot every job into its pertaining grade. An example of job classification is illustrated below.

Job Class Description for Junior Position
This class is applicable to positions that their duties require immediate supervision with clear instructions on how to follow the applicable departmental procedures with limited authority to make independent judgement.

1. Factor Comparison: this method is complex and the least used as compared to other job evaluation methods. Through this system there is a set of factors that are used to identify the worth of a job by identifying dollar value for each level of every factor. An example of factor comparison method is illustrated below.

Job	Wage Rate	Skill	Work Conditions	Effort	Responsibility
Technician	70	15	20	25	10
Safety Officer	60	15	10	15	20
Sales Rep	50	15	10	10	15
Accountant	40	10	5	5	20

Now we will highlight on the four types of the job evaluation methods (Job Evaluation Types table) in terms of their degree of subjectivity and objectivity, their frequency of use and value to the organisation as depicted in Figure 16 (Job Evaluation Methods Comparison).

Figure 17 – Job Evaluation Methods Comparison

	Objectivity	Subjectivity	Frequency of Use	Value to the organisation
Job Ranking	Low	High	High	Low
Job Classification	↓	↑	↑	↓
Factor Comparison				
Point-Factor				
	High	Low	Low	High

This comparison reemphasises how much valuable is the point-factor method to the organisations. Although it's very much reliable method because of its high validity as we mentioned before but it's not widely used in the organisations because it's difficult to administer and apply if it was run in-house which is also not so common practice. The other option which is going to third party is not also preferred because of the high costs that the companies incur when doing so. Companies that specialise in point-factor scheme implementation charge a lot of cost to apply this methodology. The details of the point factor method will be previewed now and in more details.

Point-Factor Method

This is the most common job evaluation method. It's based on a set of factors that all the jobs in the organisation are evaluated against in order to identify their relative worth. These factors are called Compensable Factors and they are extracted and identified through the job analysis process. The challenge is to establish these factors in terms of their applicability to all the jobs which means that if problem solving was identified as one of these factors then a certain level of the problem solving factor must be present at both the first level jobs like the juniors and the supervisory jobs, otherwise the resulting grading structure won't represent all the jobs fairly. Also, these factors must reflect the organisational objectives and goals.

The point factor method goes into a sequence of the following stages:

1. The first stage is to select the compensable factors. As we just said that these are the factors that we use to make a judgment on the value of the jobs. The selection process of these factors must be established based on a group opinion rather than just one individual opinion. Within this context it's advisable to make a committee that represent all the departments in the organisation in order to reflect the perspective of the organisation as a whole. These factors are elicited through referring to the available documents in HR like job analysis and job description. Again, it's very important that these factors are applicable to all the jobs in the organisation and the formation of a representative committee will help to achieve that goal. An example of these factors is complexity of work, decision making and working conditions. The number of these factors are between four and ten but there is nothing fixed when it comes to establishing this scheme. Every organisation establishes its scheme based on the needs and the job complexity it has.
2. The second stage is to establish a suitable number of levels for each factor that again represents the full organisational spectrum. The number of these levels is between four and seven. The goals of establishing these levels is to accommodate the different jobs in the scheme in terms of their complexity and how much the factor levels apply to these jobs. It's kind of a validation technique that you can use in order to examine if the factors within your scheme (The First Stage) are applicable to all the jobs or not. After that a score is assigned to each factor according to the levels intensity and how they apply to every job. The progression from one level to the other could be like this (50, 100, 150, 200, 250…etc.). An example of these levels will be highlighted on at the end of this topic.
3. The third stage is to study the jobs in the scheme through the assigned committee and to match them with the factor levels in order to assign a score for every job according to how much all the levels apply into one job. Usually a paper form (Questionnaire) should be sent to the job holder to be filled out. The result is the maximum score per each job. This is the first step toward establishing the grade structure. The result of the questionnaire should be reviewed by the direct manager and/or other committee members as appropriate.
4. The fourth stage is to evaluate all the jobs in the organisation through the assigned committee by agreeing on the job scores after filling out the job evaluation surveys. The committee double check on the factor level scores per each job to make sure that the evaluation is fair and that the evaluators didn't inflate the scores by choosing high levels for jobs that have lower level responsibilities.
5. The last step is to establish the grade structure through the rank order of the jobs after doing the complete evaluation for all the jobs with each grade containing a number of jobs that are related to each other in terms of their importance and value. These grades are then assigned to pay ranges.

* These stages are illustrated below through the following example (Job Evaluation Scheme for JTEX). It's a hypothetical example that is not real or implemented in any organisation. The purpose is to give the reader the major guidelines on how to design a point-factor scheme in reality by showing a step by step progression on the design stages.

Stage One: The Factors Selection

Job Evaluation: The Compensable Factors for JTEX

Factors	Weight	Total Score for Each Factor	No. of Levels	Score for Each Factor
Authority	10%	100	5	20
Complexity of Work	15%	150	5	30
Decision-making	10%	100	5	20
Education	5%	50	4	12.5
Impact on End Results	5%	50	5	10
People Management	20%	200	5	40
Working Conditions	15%	150	4	37.5
Problem-solving	10%	100	5	20
Work Experience	10%	100	6	17
	100%	1000		

Stage Two: A) The Factor Levels Identification and Level Scores (Weighting)

Job Evaluation – The Factors Levels for Jtex

Factors	Level / Factor Weighting						Total
	1	2	3	4	5	6	
Authority	20	40	60	80	100		300
Complexity of Work	30	60	90	120	150		450
Decision-Making	20	40	60	80	100		300
Impact on End Results	10	20	30	40	50		150
People Management	40	80	120	160	200		600
Working Conditions	37.5	75	112.5	150			375
Problem-Solving	20	40	60	80	100		300
Work Experience	17	34	51	68	85	102	357

Stage Two: B) The Factors Definitions – Examples Reflecting the First Three Factors (Authority, complexity of Work and Decision-Making)

Authority

The freedom to take action in work and authority for approving financial and business commitments.

1	Work to instructions or standards set.
2	Authority within assigned limits for a small work unit.
3	Authority within assigned limits for a functional unit.
4	Authority within assigned limits across functional units.
5	Authority for significant financial and corporate commitments.

Complexity of Work

Control over work standards, availability of guidance and support, degree of difficulties and obstacles encountered to deliver output etc.

1	Routine work processes with little training required. Operation of simple equipment. Work to instructions.
2	Work according to standards and procedures with some training required. Operation of special equipment. Under close supervision.
3	Work within specific scope of a function with general guidance. May involve supervising work of others. Require special training or proficiency in specific work area.
4	Work requiring understanding of concepts, theories, principles and practices to lead in the achievement of business goals.
5	Define goals and strategies and direct activities with broad exposure or complex practices in technical, professional or business aspects.

Decision-Making

The extent of independent judgement required.

1	Follow procedures for actions to be taken.
2	Guided by procedures but may choose alternatives.
3	Independent judgement within authority and own job scope.
4	Considerable judgement on issues linking to/impacting on other areas.

| 5 | Strategic/directional decisions with significant business impact. |

Stage Three: A) Job Evaluation Process – Jobs Matching With Factor Levels

Job Evaluation Process – Jobs Matching With Factor Levels

Position	Dep	Factors							
		Authority	Complexity of Work	Decision-making	Impact on End Results	People Management	Working Conditions	Problem-Solving	Work Experience
Logistics Officer	Finance	1	1	1	1	1	1	1	1
Store Keeper	Parts	1	2	1	1	1	3	1	1
Technician - Level 1	Service	1	2	1	2	1	3	1	1
Sales Rep - Foundational	Sales	1	2	2	2	1	2	2	2
IT System Admin	IT	1	2	2	2	1	1	3	3
Six Sigma Black Belt Engineer	Management	2	4	2	4	1	1	4	4
PSSR – Team Leader	PSSR	3	3	3	3	2	2	3	4
Service Operations Mgr.	Service	4	4	4	4	3	1	4	5
Parts Operations Mgr.	Parts	4	4	4	4	3	1	4	5
Finance Manager	Finance	4	4	4	4	4	1	4	4
HR Manager	HR	4	4	4	4	5	1	4	4

Stage Three: B) Job Evaluation Process – Jobs Matching With Factor Levels Weighting

Job Evaluation Process – Jobs Matching With Factor Levels Weighting

Position	Dep	Level / Factor Weighting								Total
Logistics Officer	Finance	20	30	20	10	40	75	20	17	232
Store Keeper	Parts	20	60	20	10	40	112.5	20	17	299.5
Technician – Level 1	Service	20	60	20	20	40	112.5	20	17	309.5
Tech Communicator	Service	20	90	40	20	40	37.5	20	34	301.5
Sales Rep	Sales	20	60	40	20	40	75	40	17	312
IT System Admin	IT	20	60	40	20	40	37.5	60	51	328.5
Six Sigma Engineer	Management	40	120	40	40	40	37.5	80	68	465.5
PSSR – Team Leader	PSSR	60	90	60	30	80	75	60	68	523
Service Operations Mgr.	Service	80	120	80	40	120	37.5	80	85	642.5
Parts Operations Mgr.	Parts	80	120	80	40	120	37.5	80	85	642.5
Finance Manager	Finance	80	120	80	40	160	37.5	80	68	665.5
HR Manager	HR	80	120	80	40	200	37.5	80	68	705.5

Stage Four: Grading Structure and Pay Range

Grading Structure	Pay Range		
	Minimum	Mid	Maximum
Senior Management			
Management			
Senior Executives/Professional			
Junior Executives/Supervisory			
Support			

Pay Structure Design

The last step after finishing the job evaluation scheme is to establish the pay structure which consists of two major parts, the grade structure and the pay ranges associated the job grades.

In the previous section specifically, the part related to Stage Three: B) Job Evaluation Process – Jobs Matching With Factor Levels weighting we reached the point where all the jobs were ranked from highest to lowest according to the maximum points granted for every job. Establishing the job grades requires the segregation of jobs according to how long the distance between jobs is.

In the previous example as related to Stage Three B let's take the store keeper job that was ranked with 299.5 points. Then let's continue our evaluation until we reached the IT system admin that was ranked with 328.5 points. You can clearly notice that the gap between the two jobs with taking into account the other jobs in between wasn't high (the net score is 29 points).

The job after the IT system admin which is the six-sigma engineer got 465.5 points with a noticeable or even big gap of 137 points (the example is not real and it's listed here just for clarification purpose). At this point it's a logical and acceptable practice to segregate the jobs starting from the store keeper through the IT system admin and to put them in one grade, after that you can begin the boundaries of a new grade.

So, by following this approach you can easily justify the segregation of jobs and groping them into grades that contain jobs of relatively equal value to the organisation. Most probably this step is being conducted by the HR department as it seems very easy to implement and justify but in order to make sure that nothing is up normal (e.g. if one job has been slotted into a grade that includes highly specialised jobs and this job has less technical weight into its composition) when it comes to finalising job grades you should make a one final review to be conducted by the job evaluation committee that would eliminate any distortion to the job grade.

The next step is to establish pay ranges that pertains to every grade. The first thing to do is to establish for the methodology that you will follow when assigning pay ranges. In principle pay ranges must be in line with the current pay rates in the market and more specifically in your industry. The goal behind that is to have competitive pay structure that you can rely on to attract talent and to retain current employees. Establishing pay ranges takes two ways, you either do it internally through relying on your expertise or you could do it externally by relying on third party consultant who specialises in external salary benchmark.

Through the first option (Internal Salary Benchmark Study) you must rely totally on your expertise on how to establish the pay ranges according to the acceptable salary benchmark standards that guarantee both a competitive pay structure and a cost effective one at the same time. Also, it's very important that you have a good network of HR colleagues who work in companies within the same industry. This aspect of the internal salary benchmark study is the major cause why most of the HR people don't prefer to do it because it takes a lot of time and effort and you could also face the refusal of some companies to provide salary data and in some cases the data you get could be wrong or not representative to the real situation. Mostly the companies you are seeking regarding the salary data are competitors so giving such data could compromise their internal brand strengths and in turn their EVP (Employees Value Proposition) stance in the market.

The second option (The External Salary Benchmark Study) is much more preferred by the HR people because it is much more valid to rely on organisations that have both technical expertise in designing grading and pay structures and the network of the benchmark companies. These companies and through their supposed reputation in the market should be able to provide you with what you need from salary data comparison details quickly and efficiently. The data you get is highly valid because the companies that have their data stored into the consultant data base do so without hesitation or fear of being exposed to other competitors. The confidentiality is very high if you went with that option. The factor that could be a disadvantage is the high cost you incur when choosing third party consultants which is of no effect when you do it in-house.

Regardless if you have chosen to do the salary benchmark internally or externally the outcome should be a salary range that consists of three salary points, the first one is the minimum salary point which is considered the starting point for all the jobs within the grade. The second one is the mid salary point and the third one is the maximum salary point.

In order to be able to identify these salary points you need to compare them with the current pay rates in the market and matching them on a scale of 100 divided into four quartiles as the following.

Figure 18 – Salary Range

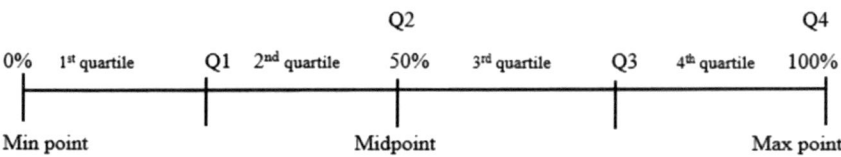

The issue of committing to these three salary points is very useful because of many considerations:

1. It establishes for a clear standard on how to assign a new employee the salary that best fit the organisation's compensation strategy. A new comer regardless of his/her expertise is usually granted the minimum salary point which both serves the new employee's expectations and the internal equity compared with employees who have relatively the same expertise. Of course, there are exceptions for highly specialised candidates who have a unique skill. In such a case you could extend the salary point up the midpoint. There are other occasions where you hire employees with long years of expertise. In this case there could be an overlap with a higher grade. It's okay to do that as long as the employee is highly qualified and is not probably going to advance vertically (promotion for a higher position). This case is rarely applied and if not managed carefully then it will lead to moral problem with the current employee in terms of their feels of inequity.
2. Having these three points divided into four quartiles will give you a leverage when taking decisions on how to move employees laterally within the same pay range. The standards upon which you will take your decision will be examined shortly.
3. When you source for new candidates for certain positions you can save time when you do your search. You will channel your search to the candidates who have salary expectations that matches your salary ranges.
4. The three salary points from a financial point of view could save you cost when you assign the salary increases based on a clear standard rather than assigning them randomly. By having these points, you will definitely have to establish for a yearly provision in your HR budget that pertains to the expected yearly salary increases as per your salary range standard.

5. Establishing for the internal equity in terms of the fairness in the salary increases issue you are contributing to the structure of your brand strategy. We mentioned before that having highly engaged employees will help in spreading a word of mouth from your current employees regarding how much the work experience in your company is enjoyable.
6. Having a consistent salary increases as per your salary range structure will enable a much more reliable salary data analytics when you aim to examine the solidity of your C&B (Compensation and Benefits) strategy. It would be much easier to predict more accurately of who is going to leave your organisation because of the unfairness in granting salary raises when you look for a three years trend that reflects consistent and comparable differences in the salary raises between employee rather than navigating through highly inconsistent and fluctuated salary raises.

These salary ranges are very important in governing the pay systems policies that we will discuss in this section. But the most critical issue is to update these salary ranges continuously in order to maintain the pay structure according to the current market pay rates. Here the element that we should trace is the yearly inflation rates within a certain geography.

Usually the inflation rates are published on many governmental websites in your region such as the central bank website. The best practice here is to update your salary ranges on a yearly basis by looking at the inflation rate for a certain year and then to multiply this rate by the salary ranges points (Min, Mid and Max) and to add the result to the salary range boundaries. This method is called again and it's widely used because of its simplicity and effectiveness in maintaining a vital pay structure. In order to complete the update process of your pay structure you must do a salary survey benchmark as we mentioned before at least once every two years. By doing that you can guarantee that your pay rates are in line with what the competitors are paying.

In summary the process of studying your pay structure is based on two sides:

1. The first one is to benchmark your pay structure (the salary ranges) with what your competitors are paying through a salary survey process (it could be done in-house or externally through a third party). The goal is to guarantee the competitiveness and the external equity of your pay structure.
2. The second one is to maintain that competitiveness by following the aging method. It's not advisable to follow only that approach and to exclude the first one, they are equally important and they complement each other. Doing the salary survey benchmark and then relying only on the aging factor to update your pay structure on the long run will result in a non-competitive pay structure. Inflation rate as a sole factor can't keep up with the salary movements within an industry

Compensation Systems

The last step after designing the pay structure is identifying the pay systems that are governed by the salary ranges. These systems are a major way that will guarantee the validity of the pay structure for relatively long periods. You don't want to adjust your pay structure according to the benchmark salary study (a process that is always time consuming and costly) and to find after two years that your salary ranges have been eroded because of inconsistent salary raises approach.

In order to preserve the validity of your pay structure you can use the following pay systems or you can use some of them according to your organisational strategy:

1. Time-Based Step-Rate Pay System: through this system the salary raises within the pay range is given based on how much time the employee has spent in a certain position. Such increases should be identified on a pre-determined basis. They are three types:

- Automatic by Percentage and Time: here the pay scale is divided into number of steps that are 3 – 7% apart. Employees with the required seniority receives one step increase. This system could work for employees at their entry-level positions up to their third year of employment. The rationale behind this is that employees within this category have almost the same performance and it's difficult to differentiate their performance level. The performance level begins to increase after the first three years which then necessitates a different approach of pay systems. There is also some type of cultures that use such systems. These cultures depend mainly on the seniority level of their employees as the main way to promote, to give salary increases or any other employment related decisions.
- Performance-Based Pay System: within this system the pay increase (time and size of the increase) is determined largely by the individual performance level of the employee. The employee receives his/her salary increase on a pre-determined basis as for the past system but the difference lies in the amount of the increase. The employee could move two steps ahead on the pay scale if the performance level was above the expectations.
- Hybrid step-rate and performance: this system is perfect as a combination of the past two systems. Here you can beat the shortcoming of both systems. Usually the employee is given automatic step-rate up to the mid-point and after that you can give performance-based pay increases until you reach the maximum. This pay system is represented in the following diagram. The main challenge here is defend the performance pay increase for an employee as you need to substantiate the reason behind the increase with fact-based evidence especially if the employee is being given two steps on the pay sale.

Figure 19 – Pay Systems

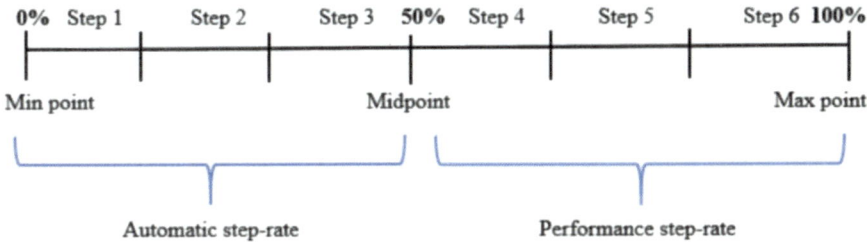

1. Performance-based pay system: this system is based on measuring the employee performance and granting him/her the related pay increase. The time and sizing of this type of pay system is linked to the performance measurement of the employee which means that the direct manager of the employee could assess the employee's performance at certain time of the year (let's say after finishing a project) and accordingly they would suggest the appropriate salary raise as per the employee's achievement. Performance considerations and the basis upon which the system is established will be discussed in the performance management section.
2. Productivity-based pay system: this system is mostly common in the industries and organisations that produce heavily tangible products. Within this system the employee is given a base wage and additional compensations based on the output produced by each individual. Let's say that the employee has received a 2000 USD for a given month as their base wage and they received additional 500 USD because they produced additional outputs above the required monthly production standard (they produced additional 250 unit × 2 USD/unit).

These pay systems are the most common between multiple pay systems and following through these systems as mentioned before will help you to establish for a robust defence against the pay increases decisions that your employer undertakes in addition to the shield you build for strong and valid pay structure that would last enough to support your long-term goals and strategies.

Compensation Systems Due Diligence

This section tackles the compensation system that we have designed in terms of its validity and strength as related to the competition and the market.

We have explained how the job evaluation methodology works in practice. The end result was a grade structure that reflects a fair distribution of jobs within the grade structure hierarchy. Once the grade structure has taken place within your total rewards structure then it's just a matter of communicating this outcome to your current employees with the least communication effort possible if the employees were involved in the process properly and from the beginning.

To a big extent the grading structure maintenance process is done less than the pay structure maintenance process. Although we hear a lot about the AI (Artificial Intelligence) and how much it is expected to change the structure of the organisations (,any jobs will be permanently replaced by machines and a big portion of the remaining jobs will need a new or even a totally different set of skills) and how the global competition is affecting drastically the current way of many business interactions. Yet we still expect that for the next few years nothing drastic will happen regarding the current job structure of most organisations which will not leave an impact on the job evaluation process.

The challenge is how to keep the other side of the compensation system (the pay structure) in line of the current market pay rates. Organisations can't easily make a decision to raise a star performer especially if their new pay rate has exceeded the maximum salary point but it would be much more easier making a decision to add a new function to their current job role. In the first one the justification for the decision is so demanding for both the executive management and the rest of the employees. The HR needs to reassure and convince the executive management that the pay structure could be externally benchmarked with the current market pay rates and accordingly to adjust the pay rates which might eliminate their fears that the pay structure has been outdated. As for the employee's colleagues you need to defend your case and to convince them through the employee's performance results which in many cases is not an easy thing to do.

In the second one the justification to add a new function to the employee's current job role is easily defended. Here you can justify the decision by referring to the expected saving in costs (in terms of not hiring a new employee) and the increased efficiency through handling two functions by one person.

In the following paragraphs I will talk about the techniques you can use to keep your pay structure within the acceptable external market pay standards. These techniques are considered to a big extent a measurement framework that you can refer to periodically or as needed when studying your pay structure.

The issue of total rewards measurement is different than the other HR functions. When you are planning for example to measure the performance management system effectiveness you begin first by establishing how the system is going to be constructed and measured then you deploy the system and after that comes the issue of the system actual measurement. You don't track the learning plans completion rate for your employee before the system starts. You must first identify the learning plan for the employee then you must wait for a certain period leaving a room for the learner to pursue his/her learning objectives then you make your measurement. In total reward the issue is different. You lay out the compensation system then you make your measurement (the benchmark with the external market pay rates) then you deploy the system. This measurement process flow for the performance management system and compensation system is illustrated below.

Figure 20 – Performance Management Measurement

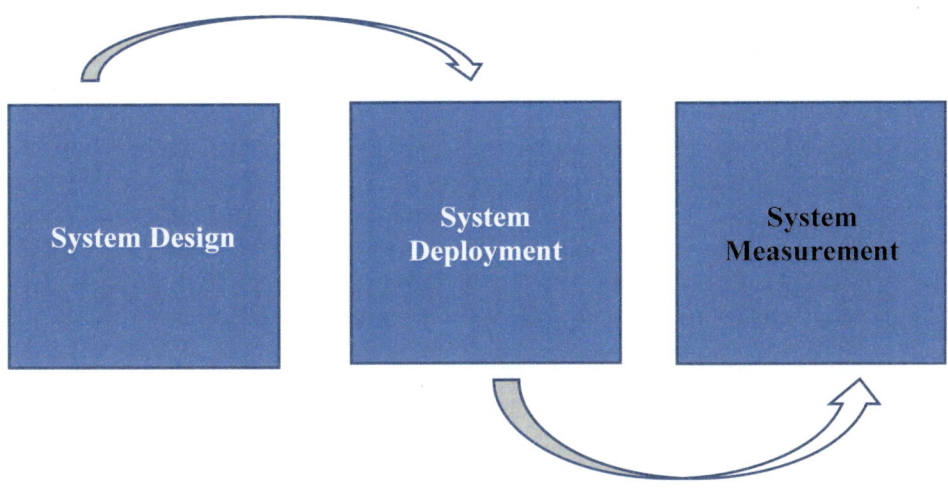

Figure 21 – Compensation System Measurement

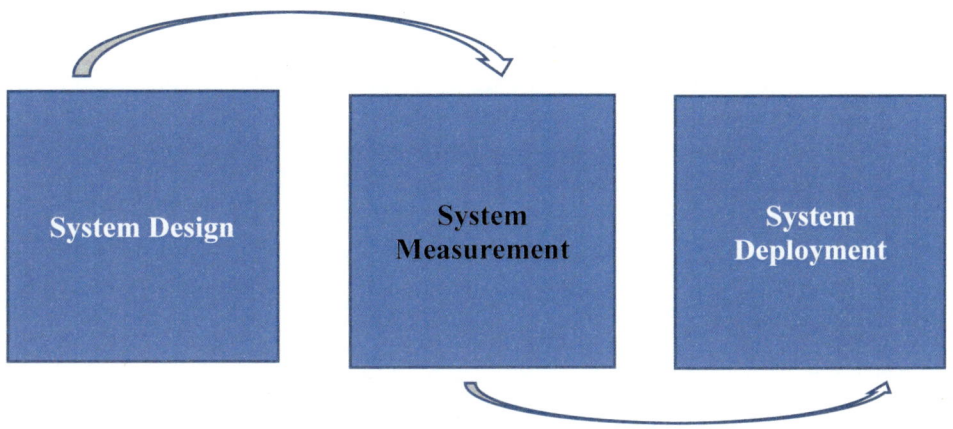

The measurement in the compensation system at the second stage is a prerequisite in order to build for the whole system competitiveness. Imagine that you do your grade structure through the point factor method and then you decide not to benchmark your current salaries with what is being paid in the market and to substitute that benchmark part of the system with assigning pay ranges that are identified haphazardly. What do you expect the result would be? One of the most important problems you will face is the distrust of the employees in your current system because in this case you don't have a reference to build upon to justify your decision. Another problem would be your inability to attract talent to your organisation because of the weak salaries you have within your compensation system.

So, this is the reason why the measurement of total rewards won't be regarded in the same way as for the other topics covered within this book.

Now we will talk about the techniques and approaches you can use to measure your compensation system effectiveness. They are the following:

1. Red-Circles Rates: these are the rates that correspond to employees who are paid more than the maximum point in the salary range. There are many reasons that could create such a problem like if one employee has been serving for a long time in a certain position with no development opportunities which made him/her stuck in one grade. In other cases, the lack of the benchmark with the market could lead to this problem leaving your salary ranges fixed while salary raises are taking place periodically which would be a cause to the red-circle rates. This problem is a big a risk to the organisation if not being acted upon instantly. In the past two cases you can provide a solution to the first one by giving additional financial incentive to the employee that would maintain the needed motivation level for the employee without affecting the grade structure maximum salary point through many salary increases to the current rate for the employees. An employee who has been working for long time in your company and has a high level of the technical expertise in his field could serve as a coach for younger employees who would benefit a lot from technical coaching from a seasoned employee. In the second case you should abide by a consistent policy that states the timing and the way to conduct a salary benchmark study in order to keep the salary ranges of your pay structure within the acceptable market pay rates.
2. Green-Circle Rates: an employee's wage rate that is below the minimum point in the salary range is considered a green-circle rate. One of the main reasons for this issue to happen is that companies could make external salary benchmark that would result in increasing the minimum salary points as a result. Another reason would be to hire a new employee who has accepted a salary below the minimum. Both ways could and should be tackled as soon as the opportunity allows for such a correction. Companies can increase the employees who became at the green-circle rate. After conducting the external salary benchmark by increasing their salaries suppose they have achieved the requirements to do so like reaching their performance goals. Rectifying this issue is much easier than the red-circles rates. It's acceptable to increase someone to the minimum salary point which would not affect the structure of the pay structure rather than increasing the employee above the maximum salary point.
3. Pay Compression: this problem happens when the difference in pay between employees is relatively small regardless of the competency level between the employees. One of the main reasons for this problem is to hire new employees who get higher pay than the current ones. Usually long-tenured employees don't get salary increases that is in line

with the prevailing market rates while new employees with less expertise would be hired with a salary higher than the current ones. This problem is called the opening salary problem. This happens because of the Inflation rates. If they happened over a span of many years then this would result in increasing the opening salaries for the new hires. Not acting upon this problem will definitely lead to moral issues with the current employees and it would definitely affect the retention rate of the new hires. When new hires see that a senior employee is being paid below the required salary point then the message delivered is the following "If I continued my employment with this company for long time then I might reach the same situation as for the senior employees who have been there for many years."

There are also other two important factors that we must think of when designing our compensation system:

- Compensation packages association with the grade structure: this point is very crucial if you want to leverage your brand efforts with the potential candidates as well as the trust level with your current employees. Throughout this point every grade within the overall company grade structure should be associated with clear TR (Total Rewards) packages that specify what every job within a certain grade is entitled for. In other words what is the basic salary for this grade, what is the bonus scheme, what is the health insurance benefit...etc. this Clarity would give you a bargaining advantage with your potential candidates as you already can convey the TR elements within your grade structure which would enhance the attraction ability for the potential candidates. Potential candidates want a high level of transparency regarding their TR packages before they enter the organisation. The same thing applies for your current employees as they would be supportive for your plans and objectives when they see that their employer is transparent with them. Also, their career aspirations would be based on a robust basis when they know what they will get when they are promoted.
- Compensation system continuous competitiveness: this point is achieved through the continuous alignment between the TR strategy and the organisational strategy. Most organisations go through different stages at their life cycle. When your organisation is at the peak you need to revise and adjust your TR structure according to that and in a way that maintains a highly attractive TR elements in your overall TR strategy in order to retain your highly valuable talent. It's well known for any HR professional who has been in the profession for several years that talented employees are an easy target for competitors when the economy is doing well. This effect is lessened when the economy is suffering but don't rest assured that you won't be in danger. Someone could argue that

how can I adjust my TR strategy without affecting the overall organisational strategy. Let's stop for a moment here. At the top of this paragraph I didn't say to adjust your TR strategy. I said to adjust your TR structure. Strategies in principle don't change holistically as they were designed first after examining the organisational reality and what the organisation really wants to achieve. In my current company the TR strategy is to be at the third quartile of the market and it has been a strategy for many years more than I can remember. When we went through an economic booming in our country few years ago, we wanted to retain our employees as well as to attract new ones. This was not possible with the current TR strategy. Moving up into the fourth quartile wasn't an option because it would harm the financial capacity of the organisation. I remember that one of the suggestions was to cut the variable incentive pay and to substitute that with high salary increases but after making some calculations we found that it would increase the financial burden for the organisation to the degree that it would harm its net profit for at least two years. Also, the suggestion of cutting the incentive pay would have also affected our EVP (Employees Value Proposition) which the incentive pay constituted an integral part of it for long time. After a long debate the suggestion that was agreed on from all the stakeholders was to rearrange the current structure of the TR. We decided to link the employee compensation with the performance rating of the employees which would help us to channel the compensation distribution in a fair way that guaranteed that high performers are being paid fairly and higher than the valued performers. This was one solution. The other solution was also to set aside a portion of the compensation budget to reward the line managers who have been a key leverage in achieving the organisational goals by giving them additional bonuses. A third solution was to reward the top salespeople of a company-sponsored personal trips rather than spending on outside the country training that would have been substituted by online training. The bottom line is that we didn't change the overall TR strategy but the elements within the TR structure were reallocated in a way that helped us a lot to keep pace with the changing economic circumstances.

Measuring TR (Total Rewards) Effectiveness

I want to highlight again that the segment related to the HR analytics within the four levels of HR excellence model (The Pinnacle) wasn't tackled separately. Before writing this book and even during writing it up to this moment I was hesitant about whether I should leave the HR analytics until I finish writing the book after covering the basic functions within the model or to embed it within the content of the book after finishing each function.

Another idea was to slow down about the HR analytics subject. Two ideas were popping up in front of my face every morning. It's a very complicated topic and maybe I should leave it to experts to write about it. Or even I can write the whole book introducing the key topics and after few years I can supplement it with this segment, the analytics segment. The goal was to give the reader the time to digest and understand the main topics without adding the complexity of the analytics topic.

I decided that I must include the analytics topic from the beginning. After all I am not writing a multiple parts novel that should include suspense. The reader must have a full grasp of the topic and that won't happen if I separated the two topics from each other. I decided also to follow a consistent sequence by adding the analytics topic after each function to avoid any disconnect in the content and/or the ideas stream that the reader must not experience.

Another concern that I am sure many readers will have is their thoughts about the comprehensiveness of the HR analytics subject covered within this book. Someone could argue that the HR analytics is a much wider topic than the content presented within this book. It's about building relevant data base through which you can extract data anytime without exerting the traditional effort of gathering data from multiple sources then trying to conciliate the data in order to have it in a useful format. Yes, it is.

It's also about tracking patterns in a set of similar data for multiple years and trying to discover the logic behind the data then predicting a certain outcome for the future. Yes, it is also true. But for the purpose of this book I previewed a basic level of the HR analytics. I stated earlier that this book is dedicated for HR professionals at their early career stage so my purpose was to bring to their attention the key elements of a successful HR department by introducing the four levels of HR excellence.

The measurement framework that I introduce within this book was not so comprehensive and I have done that on purpose. It's better to understand what are the key success factors for an effective HR department and to apply them successfully rather than going deep into the complexity of the HR analytics topic and getting nowhere (you can capture that knowledge from other sources once you advanced your career). Can you imagine that you can excel at the recruitment function by only developing your skills about the recruitment metrics without first advancing your sourcing strategy which will lead you eventually to the right measurement framework? Of course not. You need first to master the basics then you can move to a higher level of HR excellence.

I believe that it was necessary to mention the aforementioned at this stage of the book before going further. My goals were to illustrate more the structure of the book as I planned for.

Now let's talk about the TR (Total Rewards) measurement framework. In the previous topic (the compensation system due diligence) I talked about how to maintain an effective pay structure. This area is very important as a transactional step toward a comprehensive strategic total reward effective system. In order to capture the effect of your total reward strategy on the overall organisational effectiveness you must identify what are the areas you believe are making a difference into your organisation.

There are organisations that measure the effect of their total rewards systems on employee's engagement, others could relate their TR system to applicable country wage laws. In the first one the engagement could be a key driver for the organisation's success if the company has a differentiation strategy, in the second one the organisation might be operating in a country were many factors like employee engagement is considered minor as compared to other more valued factors like how much the organisation is compensating its employees as per the prevailing wage laws.

The organisational factors that you can link your TR strategy with are numerous but again you need to be thoughtful about what must be measured. Trying to measure everything will increase the burden of your measurement efforts and could lead you to analysis paralysis. It will prevent you also from targeting your investment to the right channels in terms of the HR strategies and initiatives that will yield the best return on investment.

I have seen a lot of literature about total rewards but not that much was written about the measurement side of total rewards. I guess that companies focus more on other impactful areas of HR like managing employees' performance as they believe the impact of such areas is much more strategic. To a great extent this is true but the problem is that companies forget that total rewards comprise a big portion of the organisational HR yearly budget so if not managed well the impact won't be as expected. You can consider the salaries, sales commissions, health insurance benefit you provide to your employees as a necessary evil and in such case you will not pay attention to the effect they might yield and thus you will consider them as no more than expenses to be managed by cutting them down or you could consider these elements as a key strategic factor to your success and then you will dedicate the resources and time to measure how much TR strategy is helping you to achieve your goals. That's the reason why companies shouldn't overlook this very important area, the main issue is how you perceive TR; is it a strategy to be optimised or a budget to be monitored.

The TR measurement model in Figure 17 that I will introduce is supposed to boost your TR strategy. It includes many factors that are essential to the success of any organisation and you can also pick and choose from that model as per your needs. The model elements are distributed over three segments but these segments are not to be followed in a sequence. You can begin from any segment you want as long as you are aligning these elements to your overall organisational strategy. For the purpose of facilitating the model execution I have arranged it in that way. It's much easier to digest the model in a segmented way rather than trying to implement its elements as a bulk. The TR measurement model is illustrated below:

Figure 22 – The TR Measurement Model

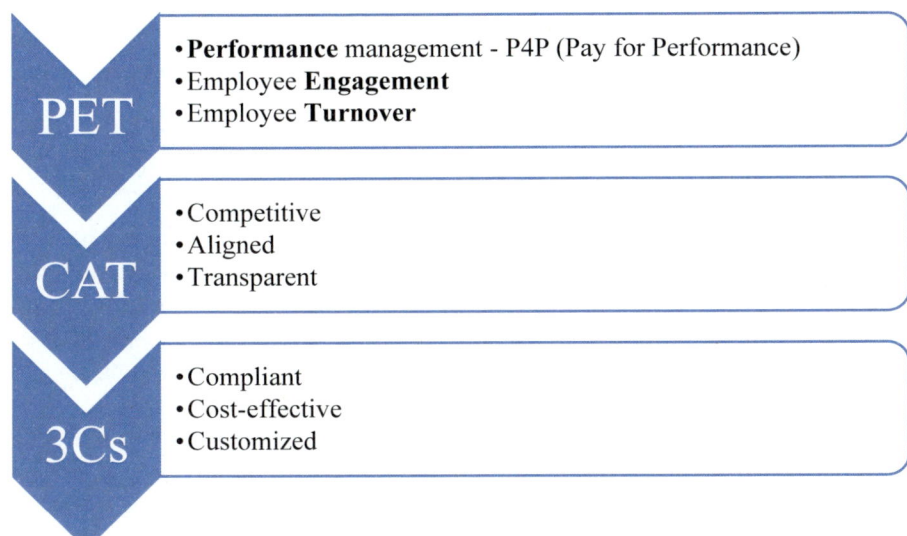

The First Segment and which I called PET represents three areas and they are Performance Management, Employee Engagement and Employee Turnover.

Performance Management or P4P (Pay for Performance) is one of the most important HR functions and this system has a clear link with total rewards. Most of the performance management systems that really work in reality do so because of rewarding the employees who have achieved their goals. So, rewards are a supportive factor in the success of performance management system and that's why you need to pay attention to the link between performance management and total rewards.

Measuring the effectiveness of your total rewards systems as related to performance management has two facets:

- The first point is to track the satisfaction of high performers regarding their rewards as an outcome after the performance appraisal process. Do they believe they were rewarded fairly? Did the rewards they got are equitable compared to their efforts? Paying for performance must be categorised as per the performance level of employees, each segment of the performance ranks (satisfactory, excellent, extraordinary...etc.) must have an associated compensation percentage in order to achieve the required satisfaction level of your overall rewards systems.
- Do the total rewards include other items that could be linked with performance management other than the compensation like providing training opportunities? This variety in TR enhance the effectiveness of your performance management system in terms of the flexibility of taking many decisions upon the outcome of the performance review.

Your ability to gather valid data regarding the past two points and the ability to analyse it is an indication that your total rewards strategy is effective.

The second point is the **Employee Engagement**. This is the most common approach to measure your total rewards system effectiveness. Through this point you dedicate a segment within your engagement survey to ask your employees about their opinions regarding the TR elements. Someone could argue that it's time saving to measure the TR system through engagement only rather than spending time and effort on multiple frontiers.

Here there are two points. First is the availability of budget and resources to do the engagement survey which could be a factor that prevents a lot of us to do it. The second point is that engagement gives you only a high-level information so the variety of TR measurement approaches that we are discussing now will open a lot of new opportunities to identify the effectiveness of your TR system.

Employees' Turnover is the third point in the PET segment. Many people track the turnover percentage on a monthly basis without digging deep into the details or the triggers of turnover. Turnover percentage alone won't reveal anything unless you explore in a systematic way the reasons behind turnover. Within this context there are two ways to explore the reasons behind turnover. They are the exit interview and the stay interview.

Through the well-known exit interview approach, you ask the person in a paper-based or online format a series of questions asking about many employment topics within which total rewards is a key area. In order to make sure that total rewards are a factor in employee turnover or not you need to detect the trend of your exit interview analysis over the span of a certain period. I remember clearly and not going back in time so much that when we conducted the exit interview for our company the discovery of the main drivers of turnover took us three years of pattern detecting.

For a period of three years the main reason for the turnover was getting an offer from other companies with higher salary. The main reason for that was the absence of a salary increase policy as part of the remuneration and benefits segment in the exit interview analysis which led many employees to search for other companies that can provide that. The results for the exit interview for my company is illustrated in the below graph (Exit Interview Visualisation – Top 5 Reasons for Leaving).

The second approach is the stay interview. As the name implies your main role here as an HR professional is to extract the reasons that could force the employee to leave beforehand rather than waiting until the employee leaves and then trying to discover the truth. In the first one you're being a proactive HR person while in the second one (Exit Interview) you are reactive which means that most probably you will not be able to make a difference. I've heard from the employees who left my organisation when I was doing with them the exit interview over and over the same sentence "why did you wait until now to ask me why I am leaving."

Acting upon the outcome of the past two areas is very important for you if you want to increase the effectiveness of your total rewards systems as related to turnover. It's also worth mentioning here that turnover analysis is interconnected with all the employment aspects you have within your organisation. Through the below graph it was clear that total rewards were a determinant factor in the turnover rate but in other organisations the factors affecting turnover could differ to reach many other areas.

Figure 23 – Exit Interview Visualization – Top 5 Reasons for Leaving

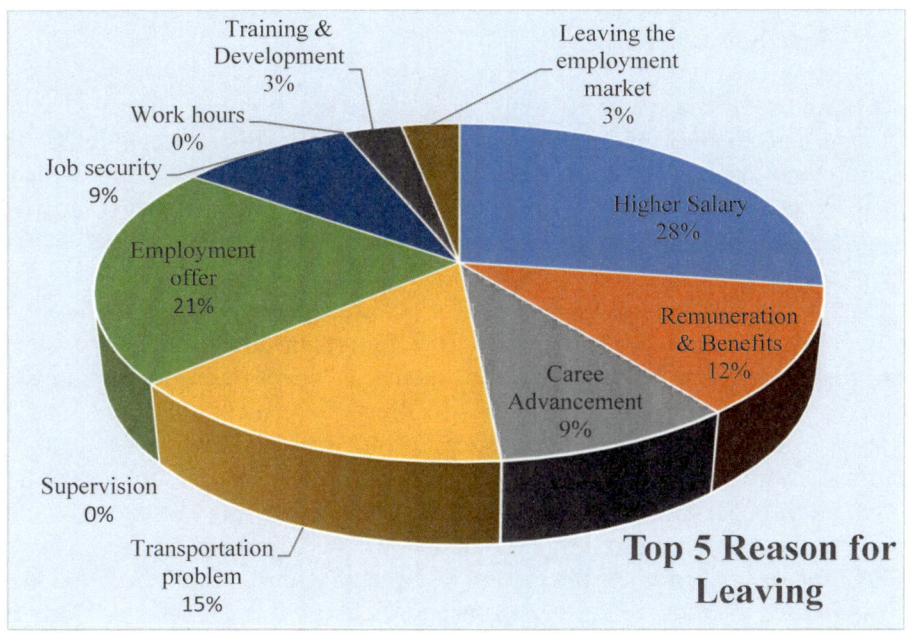

The Second Segment (CAT) represents competitive, aligned and transparent. The details of these three elements are explained below.

Competitiveness has been covered indirectly in the compensation system design section. Again, we will summarise what needs to be done to have a TR competitive strategy:

1. You need first to compare your TR elements with the external market in terms of their competitiveness. This could be done through benchmarking your TR elements with selected companies in your industry to gauge how much they are close, match or far away from your competitors. This process must be done regularly in order to keep your TR structure live and thriving. The more your total rewards systems are in line with the market the more you are able to attract and retain your best talent.
2. The other equal issue that is also very important is the internal competitiveness of your TR system. By this I mean how much your TR system has the ability to advance your other HR strategies? If some

employees aspire to climb the managerial ladder, does your total rewards support that? Does it provide elements that encourage high potentials to advance their careers like the appropriate learning opportunities or the needed global assignments to develop the cultural intelligence competency? It's equally important to have a TR strategy that is both externally and internally competitive. What's the value of having a highly external competitive compensation system through which you can attract high potentials while internally the TR system does not retain these high potentials?

Aligned total rewards has been discussed in the previous chapter. I talked how you can change the structure of your total rewards strategy rather that changing the strategy in order to keep the needed alignment level with the organisational strategy without holistically making big changes that could affect the principles behind your TR strategy (the TR philosophy and guiding principles).

From a broader perspective your total rewards system must go in line with the overall organisational perspective. If your organisational leaders aspire to serve their customers with a high and intensified level that your organisation didn't witness before then you need to reflect these aspirations on your TR strategy. Commission rates for salespeople must be adjusted in a way that it becomes competitive in order to motivate the salespeople to serve their customers as needed and a portion of their commissions must be geared toward achieving that goal measured by the satisfaction level of the customers.

The major goal of your TR system alignment with the organisational goals is to guarantee the most effective results and yield of your TR system. Many HR leaders' fails to recognise the business reality in terms of what is really the vison and the mission of the organisation are about. This lack of understanding affects the TR system negatively. The issue here is not your TR system in itself. If you refer to other HR books or sources you will find that the structure of TR in most organisations is similar in terms of the design principles and the TR elements. The excellence of your TR systems and strategy is based on how you are able to gear your TR systems toward achieving the organisational goals.

Transparency is the third element of the CAT category. I mentioned in the introduction for this section that the transparency effect of TR begins high when a new employee joins the organisation and this effect fades slowly as the employee has merged into the organisation starting from the principle that employees appreciate more the intangible elements of their employment experience like how much recognition they receive for doing their job well.

But this is not to confuse that the effect of TR is of utmost importance and must be maintained at an acceptable level regardless of the conditions. I think that most of us are motivated to do our jobs well if our psychological needs were met. Some of us will excel at what they do if they were part of a team while others' motives could be related to how much authority they have over their subordinates. But in the two cases none of us would keep the same level of motivation if our salaries and the other benefits we had were affected negatively.

Being transparent requires that HR should keep the same level of communication with the employees regarding their TR packages regardless of the organisational conditions. If you were honest with your employees regarding the reasons for the cut in their compensation packages because of the bad economic conditions then you might gain their trust and you won't need to make changes to your compensation policies in a drastic way that could affect your organisation's financial situation.

At this moment and while I am writing this book my variable compensation was reduced almost 40% and taking into account that this variable element of my TR package was comprising 40% of my total compensation package the effect was negative on my financial well-being. But to be honest with myself I don't feel any bad feelings regarding that cut in my income. The approach that we used with the whole company including myself was to make a gradual cut in the variable compensation for a 12-month period so the employees won't experience this big cut in their compensation suddenly and without preparation.

The other important element was the instant communication with the employees regarding the details of their cut though their managers. Communication was the most important element in the whole issue. Without it we would never have the ability to make that move.

The other issue in a transparent TR strategy is to maintain this transparency all the times regardless of the organisational conditions. This requires for example publishing the pay structure boundaries to your employees and even some companies have taken a further step by making the salary details for the employees accessible for anyone but this high level of transparency requires a high level of trust between the employees and the organisation so these information won't be used for personal purposes form some employees like trying to destroy the morale of the organisation by spreading info to others about a possible inequity in the income distribution.

The level (how much information is revealed from the TR packages in the organisation) and degree (who is authorised to access what information) of transparency are pure organisational concerns but what is important is to be transparent when it comes to TR strategy regardless of the level and degree of transparency. Although transactional in its nature TR could affect the strategic capability of the organisation if not managed well and as per the previous recommendations.

Measuring the previous two points (Alignment and transparency) could be done by making opinion survey for the senior management about their satisfaction from the TR alignment with the organisational goals and by making company-wide scale survey asking the employees about their opinions and satisfaction on the TR transparency policy.

The Last Segment is the 3Cs. Three Cs consists of three elements:

Compliance is the first element; this is the most straightforward point within the whole model. Here HR people must exert the required due diligence to align their TR elements with the local applicable laws. Countries have different base wage considerations that companies must abide by. There are also the retirement benefits that vary greatly according to each country's laws and regulations.

Companies that abide by the applicable laws are always in the safe side against any legal claims from the employees or against any governmental audits or check-ups. But these companies must pay attention again to the competitiveness factor of their TR. They must apply the principles covered in the competitiveness segment in order to keep pace with the market conditions.

It won't differentiae your position as an employer of choice if you just followed the applicable wage laws into your region. This could work with the new comers who don't have an extensive or long experience. But in the long run you need to support that with other elements like the competitiveness and by linking the pay with the performance in order to maintain an effective TR structure. If you look closely at the TR measurement model you will notice that the elements within the model are interrelated with each other.

Paying for performance is a key example here. If you granted your employee a financial incentive without being transparent on the reasons that made you to pay that incentive then this could question your decision regarding if the pay was equal to the effort exerted from the employee.

Another example would be the employee turnover. If you found through the exit interview that some departments are experiencing high turnover rate because of the weak compensation policy in your organisation and if you directed your action plan targeting these departments only then you are unintentionally excluding other departments that are facing engagement problems for the same reason.

It could be that turnover till the moment has not emerged in these departments. But it doesn't mean that it's not coming, it's just a matter of time. Here you need to compliment your exit interview findings through targeting the organisation as a whole by making engagement a company-wide scale effort through which you can make sure you are not excluding anyone. This interrelation is important for you to understand if you want digest the model and to apply its elements successfully.

Cost-Effectiveness is another important factor in the 3Cs segment. This element is about providing pay and benefits that are attractive for the new comers and the potential candidates without affecting the financial ability of the organisation. You could spend big amount of dollars on a yearly basis trying to motivate your workforce but to find later that what you are paying is not getting you anywhere but to increase the financial burden of the organisation and the motivation level has not increased.

Again, understanding the interrelation of the whole model will help you to target your workforce with a highly recognised TR package. Paying for performance has a multidimensional effect on the TR measurement model including the cost-effectiveness element. If you allocate the financial payments assigned within your budget according to the performance level then you will guarantee a high positive effect in terms of the outcome of your total rewards.

Giving generous salary increases to your high potentials will enhance the organisational performance while on the other hand if the salary raises are granted subjectively without relating them to the performance level of your employees then this will affect negatively the whole organisation. It doesn't make sense to reward two employees with the same salary increases while one of them has made exceptional performance. Also, from a financial point of view this case is a representation of a less than optimal budgetary management approach.

I would like to consider the cost-effectiveness topic as an approach to reflect upon when looking at the other elements into your TR measurement model. You can consider it as a starting point in order to establish for a more robust TR measurement approach.

Establishing for a **Customised** Total Rewards structure is the last point in the whole model regarding the measurement of your TR strategy effectiveness. We relate this segment to the demographics into your organisation. Every ingle organisation has a multi-generational workforce. There are the baby-boomers, X Generation, Y Generation and the techno savvy generation (The Z generation) who is almost ready to enter the workforce.

Every generation has its own unique needs and by all means you need to link and customise your TR offerings as per these generational segments and needs. Baby boomers who are about to retire pay more attention to their retirement plans and how their employer could enhance them before they retire, the Y generation is aspiring to climb the managerial ladder and they want their voice to be heard from their superiors.

X generation are well respected in their organisations but they probably want a much wider effect on the new generations by acting the role of mentors and coaches for these generations. The highly interactive and complicated life style we are going through now requires a totally different TR offering for the Z generation like providing an advanced technology in the workplace in order to grasp their attention and thus retaining them like the virtual workplace technology.

Tracing these different TR needs is doable throughout your annual engagement survey. An advance analysis of your engagement survey findings should include the demographic analysis through which you can consider the variant needs of the different generations within your workplace. In the first engagement surveys we conducted in my company we discovered that a big portion of the X generation had a concern regarding the training opportunities they should have. It was a little bit weird at first. How come that an experienced generation who has been in the workforce long enough would be concerned about their training opportunities?

What we thought were for granted (Xers are experienced enough and don't need that much training like the new generations) was never the case. These people wanted to feel their importance and existence in the workplace and providing them with ample training opportunities was a reaffirmation that this segment of the workforce is very important to the whole organisation.

Following on the above model (TR measurement model) is not a sure recipe for success. You need to study the model elements carefully in order to deploy what best works for you. You need also to integrate this model with the overall organisational HR measurement model you have in order to maximise your outcome. An aggregated HR measurement model will help you to establish a wide range of results that benefit the organisation as a whole rather than targeting fragmented HR measurements.

Employment Brand: Introduction

The third part of the foundational level of the HR excellence is the employment brand. This segment of the model has an utmost importance and impact on both the recruitment effectiveness and the employee engagement. Employees' engagement as I see it is an inevitable result of the brand strategy of the organisation and this will be discussed later on. As an outcome of the employment brand employee engagement will lead also to better employee retention as illustrated in the HR excellence model.

The four levels of HR excellence model represent the relationship between the HR functions within the model in a sequential way that helps the reader to build an effective HR department without going into the confusion of what area to tackle first. In the model (at the beginning of the book) you can notice that all the functions within the four levels starting from the foundational through the pinnacle are illustrated visually as an extension to every level, e.g. the advanced level is followed by the succession management function through a one side arrow.

This relationship applies to the whole model except for the employment brand function, you will notice that the relationship between the employment brand and the rest of the functions in the foundational level (total rewards and recruitment) is reciprocal represented by a two-sided arrow. This means that the functions at the foundational level are affected by each other.

Can you imagine an effective recruitment sourcing strategy that can feed your talent pipeline effectively without an effective brand effort for your organisation? Of course, not if we accounted for the drastic talent shortage worldwide. Can you also guarantee that your best in class compensation system is well recognised for the candidates out there if your brand efforts are not enough? Of course not. An effective employment brand will impact the other functions positively. This is a one side if the reciprocal relationship between the brand and the other elements. The other side is the effect of recruitment and total rewards on the employment brand.

Simply stated if your recruitment strategy and total rewards are not of big value to your organisation what do you think the effect will be on your employment brand? You will find that there are big numbers of candidates who want to join your organisation but the potential that they will really join your organisation is not high. It could be either that your selection tests had validity problems which made you to select the wrong hires or that your TR packages were not appealing to the candidates after they joined your organisation. In both cases your credibility will be damaged that any future brand efforts will not be that much successful.

I remember very much when we began our brand efforts as a support for our expansion in the mining business. Extensive actions exerted to support our brand efforts to attract capable and qualified technicians. After several months of a systematic and consistent branding we were able to attract a big number of technicians. As we usually do all the candidates had to go through a robust selection procedure including a knowledge-based test that was designed specifically to identify the knowledge level for these candidates.

There were three levels of tests. Starting from first level technicians to the senior technicians. As part of our strategy and as we want to have best of the best technicians, we conducted the highest-level test for the candidates. The result was that almost no one passed the test or even reached an acceptable score. After that we witnessed a decline in the number of candidates who applied for a technician job. We heard from a lot of the prospective candidates whom we were approaching that the tests we administer are very difficult and no one could possibly pass them. There was a psychological barrier that we created with no intention to do that.

After studying the whole situation and taking into account the weakness of the vocational training outcomes in our country we realised that a quick action must be taken. In order to rectify the situation, we lowered the level of the tests from the highest level to the first level. The results were astonishing. The scores of candidates were much higher than before and in turn the number of potential candidates increased. Of course, the variation in the knowledge level was a very important consideration and the plan to compensate for that variation was through the accelerated apprenticeship program we have created.

In summary the gap in our recruitment function and specifically the selection procedure has disrupted our brand efforts and could have led to more acute effect if we didn't rectify the whole situation. So, employment brand, recruitment and total rewards are all equal in terms of their effect on each other and a seasoned HR professional must account for that reciprocal effect when working on the foundational HR level.

We mentioned before in the recruitment topic that the role of recruiters has changed dramatically. They are now marketers who promote for their organisation's employment. Shifting to that modern role of recruitment marketing requires a change in the mindset of the people who take care of the recruitment issues.

Theses recruiters must understand the role they are seeking to fill in terms of the strategic value the role is bringing to the organisation and how to convey that message to the candidates in the market in order to grasp their attention. It's just like when a marketing professional is making marketing campaign for a new product by touching on the value this product will bring to the customers as compared to the competition.

This new role requires also a robust partnership with the senior management to understand the organisation's value proposition and how to convey that value into tangible recruitment actions. Also, a new concept has taken place in the recent years. It's the CRM (Candidates Relationship Management) which holds us as HR professionals the accountability to build a continuous relationship with the talent in the marketplace in order to bring any needed talent quickly and without any burden.

This variation on the traditional recruitment role had its effect on creating the new function of employment brand that became very necessary to support the continuous efforts of any organisation in attracting and retaining the needed talent. Employment brand is an emerging HR function which means that no clear structure for this function is yet developed although there are some metrics that some organisations have in place to measure the effectiveness of their brand efforts.

Of these metrics is the yield ratio of the candidates who applied online after participating in a job fair. Other organisations might follow the number of likes for the company page on Facebook and LinkedIn from the potential candidates after a marketing campaign although these metrics if not analysed further, their outcome is not an indication that your employment brand is effective. Getting 2000 likes on your company's LinkedIn page doesn't meant that all the candidates are really interested to join your organisation. These candidates' behaviour triggers to join your organisation is much more complicated to track than dealing with commodity customers in which their purchasing behaviour is tracked easily.

During the upcoming pages we will cover the employment brand topic within three common phases (The Employment Brand Model) and they are the employment brand strategy design, employment brand strategy execution and the employment brand strategy evaluation. Under each segment there are the elements that comprise the employment brand model. The model is illustrated in Figure 17. The model is illustrative of the key elements that must be available in any employment brand function in order to be considered effective and will be discussed in the upcoming pages.

Figure 24 – The Employment Brand Model

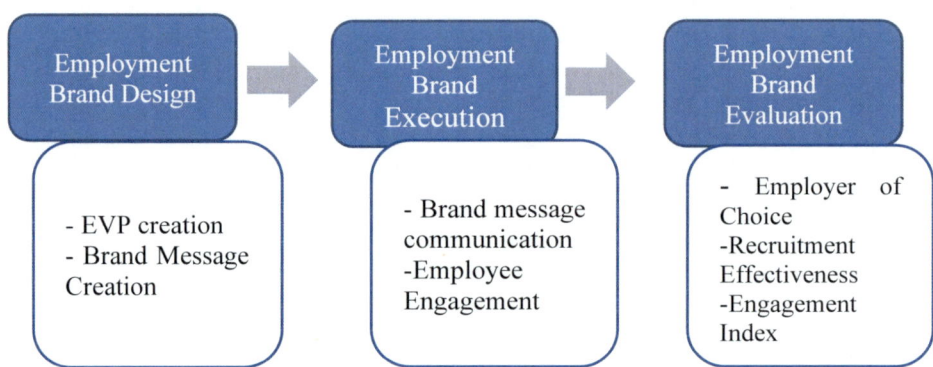

Employment Brand Design

We mentioned that the current role of any recruitment professional is to promote for the organisation's key strengths to the outside in order to attract the talent that the business needs. So gone are the days when workforce planning was purely focused on satisfying the internal business needs (line managers' needs) in terms of the required numbers of employees and the required skills that they should possess.

This is not to underestimate this traditional role of the recruitment function but historically following only through this transactional role of recruitment has fallen short. In order to have a complete picture of your recruitment function you need to look also for the outside. Here I am talking about the prospective candidates. These are the ones whom you are trying to convince to join your organisation.

Long time ago marketing professionals in many companies were focused on pushing their products to the consumers hoping that they will attain their sales targets. But these companies have realised that this approach will not create the market position that they aspire to accomplish so they moved to another totally different approach. It was about pulling the consumers to their products rather than pushing the products through creating a compelling image about the value of their products through for example the TV ads and many other marketing channels.

The same approach applies for the recruiters in their organisations. An effective recruiter needs to balance the internal recruitment needs of their organisations with the external demands of the potential candidates. This is the essence of employment brand effective strategy. It's about understanding the business needs and matching these needs with the potential candidates' desires and aspirations. In other words, you need to create an effective work environment that retains the current employees while also attracts the potential candidates.

How can we create that balance? In order to achieve that balance, you need to work on creating your **EVP (Employees Value Proposition)** and in turn creating your brand message. Let's first talk about the EVP (Employee Value Proposition). What does it mean? And how we can maintain an effective EVP despite of the fierce talent competition in the market?

EVP (Employees Value Proposition) is the value that you create for your employees in terms of the employment conditions, benefits, rewards and any other areas of interest to them that other companies in your industry can't provide or compete against. Many companies struggle for many years trying to discover how to create an effective EVP but without any potential for success or in many cases with limited success. Why is this happening?

The inherent nature of most businesses all over the world has been focused for many decades on the tangible outcomes of their businesses in terms of the revenue or net profits they should gain, this focus has inhibited the many attempts of the new management paradigm advocates represented in the modern HR function to establish for the intangible side of the business. Her I am talking about the human capital side of any business.

No organisation can sustain its productivity and the long-term well-being without its people. They are the engine that generates the power needed for any organisation. Starting from this premise HR function has evolved until it became strategically focused on serving their businesses in achieving their overall goals and objectives through their most precious assets, their employees. From here also started the value creation concept that we will focus on during this chapter.

Creating the promised value that business leaders are aspiring to have is not an easy job at all, it requires understanding the importance of human capital investment and its expected impact on business. It requires also to understand that investing in your human capital takes a lot of effort and time in terms of the performance improvement planning for your employees and most importantly to believe that any return on investment made in your human capital is going to take time before you reap the benefits.

The business leaders who believed in the human capital investment have moved many steps ahead in terms of creating competitive advantage as compared to their peers. They believe that creating the most desirable value for their employees must begin by focusing on the individual needs of their employees and how to satisfy them. They have taken the satisfaction issue many steps father until they reached to the employee engagement concept creation.

Employee engagement is the long-term strategy that focuses both on satisfying the short-term needs of the employees (e.g. salaries and benefits) and the long-term needs represented in creating a better employer-employee trust and thus establishing for a longer employment relationship. From the employee engagement concept starts the EVP creation which is the essence of the employment brand.

As a key rule that you need to follow from now on regarding your employment brand is that any current attempt or any future attempt to establish for your employment brand effectiveness should begin from within the organisational boundaries. By that I mean by referring to your employees and to communicate with them in what way works for them in order to understand the triggers that are appealing and motivating for them.

Engagement and employment brand go with each other. In fact, they complement each other. Your employees are your ambassadors to the outside. If they are engaged, they are the ones who will talk positively about their organisation. Here we refer to the well-known marketing approach through the word of mouth. It doesn't matter if you participate in a dozen job fairs every year trying to polish your organisation's image while your employees are not engaged.

You need to maintain a balance between these two elements (Employee Engagement and Employment Brand) all the times in order to guarantee that what you are trying to convey to the outside matches what's happening in the inside. If you say to your prospective candidates that your senior management supports the open-door policy and the reality is totally the opposite of what you are saying then there is inconsistency between these two elements which in turn will affect your long-term ability to enhance your talent pipeline if that was your main goal behind your employment brand strategy.

We said that employee engagement is the key to an effective brand but what is the real value of undertaking engagement surveys as a driver of the employment brand. Engagement surveys if were managed effectively can open the door for you as an HR professional to know about the triggers that are most important to your employees which will help you to create your EVP but the main problem with the employee value proposition that many companies propose is the gap between what the employees want and what their organisations are proposing to them.

It's a big mistake to prepare a list of the benefits or advantages that you intend to offer to your employees and to consider these as the final EVP elements. The main problem that I witnessed during many years of working in HR is not the EVP itself. EVP is an appealing factor for both the current employees and the prospective ones. The problem lies in the way the business executives want the EVP to be. They think that C&B (Compensation and Benefits) packages as dictated by their agendas is more than enough when it comes to an appealing EVP.

They forget that what's really important is not the lengthy list of the C&B elements or how shiny they are (e.g. having a free club membership). What's really important is how genuine you are when you are designing your C&B packages as the path to an effective EVP. By that I mean that proposing the EVP should be linked with the employee engagement survey outcomes. Employees expresses their concerns transparently through engagement survey. So, they should be the starting point when designing your EVP.

It's better to include a work/life balance policy in your EVP rather than giving your employees the free club membership if the W/L balance was an area of concern that you discovered in your engagement survey. A thoughtfully designed engagement survey can reveal a wealth of information through which you can extract the key elements of your EVP. There are a lot of engagement survey models that you can refer to and here I am mentioning one of the best models I've ever seen. It's Hay Group – Korn Ferry's model.

This model contains many questions that were designed to elicit the true factors of engagement that any company must focus on. It also gives you the feature of benchmarking your engagement findings with other similar organisations. This is just an example on one key engagement survey tool that can help you to save time when pursuing such initiative. Here I mean the time you expend while trying to understand the engagement triggers of your employees.

Also, a key area to look for when conducting the engagement surveys is how much your employees are really involved in the EVP design. Conducting the survey in itself won't answer your EVP questions, it's just the starting point. You need, through an inclusive focus group, to have the feedback of your employees on the reasons why they have made a certain judgement throughout the survey. Relying on the leadership trust score for the marketing department in your survey only won't give you a clear picture about what it means. Unless you probe on the reasons for a certain score in the engagement survey in a detailed and comprehensive way then most probably you will not get a true answer. So much involvement in the whole engagement experience is required in order to validate the engagement survey scores.

After you have finished identifying your EVP elements based on your engagement drivers now it's the time to draft a tailored **Brand Message** through which you can convey the organisational value to your employees and the potential candidates. This message doesn't have to be a long statement nor does it have to be something formal that you publish on your website. The most important thing is to live the brand so you can create the brand identity that motivates your workforce. Of course, there should be building blocks upon which all the other brand elements reside.

Employees and potential candidates value a lot of things ranging from the tangible elements in their employment contract like the salaries and the direct benefits to the intangible elements like the W/L balance. It's not rational to list them all on your website. Imagine that you have listed a dozen of the EVP elements on your website. Do you think that this will attract the potential candidates you aspire to have in your workforce? It could be, but most probably you won't get the attention of the high potential candidates who really search for the unique proposition that distinguishes you from others.

It's more effective to list on your website the main cultural theme you have as an attraction factor rather than listing the traits of your culture. It's expected and common to mention that you provide career progression opportunities as part of your culture but it would be more powerful to mention the following statement "we foster a transformational way of leading our employees and thus enabling them to transfer their careers through their own choices." For sure that anybody who reads this statement would be attracted to know more about the organisation.

So, it's about being concise and up to the point when it comes to the brand message.

The brand message is changeable. This does not mean that your key EVP elements (your identity) is changeable also. The identity of a human being, that is his/her psychology is constant and won't change regardless of how much a person has advanced in his/her experiences. An introverted person who is reluctant to voice their concerns in a business meeting will remain so even after ten years of her tenure in the organisation but a key difference in their personality could be the easiness of their interventions in a business meeting as compared with their personality in the past.

The same applies for your EVP. Your culture as a key EVP component is mostly constant and won't change over the years. If innovation is a key component within your culture then it will not change even if you adopted a new business model. What you could change within the culture could be the way how innovation is dealt with. In the past new ideas could have taken time to go live going through the business hierarchies while now the time taken of the new ideas development and execution is much faster after R&D function has been decentralised at each business unit.

Brand message as the intermediary between the brand design and brand execution should be and will remain constant in principle but the way it appears to the outside is changeable. At times of the business booming you could use promotional videos featuring your internal work environment through employees' testimonial as a way to grasp the attention of the biggest number possible of candidates while in the periods of the economic recession you could stop such videos or keep them to the lowest degree possible in order to keep the balance between the brand efforts and the workforce requirements.

Here you can use other approaches to remain in touch with the market. You could for example do on campus recruitment campaigns with the local schools in the market when you are in need of attracting new candidates. Here you are satisfying your recruitment needs specifically with targeted approach that will help you to remain vigilant regarding the candidates' movement in the market and at the same time you won't jeopardise your credibility by attracting big numbers of candidates without the potential to hire from them even on the short run.

Also, one of the areas that many companies are using to broaden their brand expansion is the diversity they plan for as part of their brand strategy. Diversity has developed over many years. It was basically focused on how diverse an employer is in terms of including different employees in its workforce in terms of the colour, religion, origin and many other factors. The concept has changed dramatically because the diversity in its old concept didn't guarantee anything but the outside variations we have mentioned.

Because of the pressing business demands and what they have brought over in terms of the huge global competition and the negative impact on the organisational ability to attract talented employee, most organisations shifted to another dimension of the diversity. They preserved the traditional concept but they have expanded the concept by introducing an amended definition of the diversity. It's about attracting diverse employees with different origins but at the same time to admit that to excel at your diversity strategy you need to accept the different mindsets of these people. To accept their different backgrounds and how they have shaped their thinking.

Diversity as defined in this concept has the utmost impact on enhancing your brand effectiveness and ultimately will impact your recruitment effectiveness. This is not to undermine that there are many other elements you can use to enhance your brand strategy but diversity is one of the areas that if taken advantage of will accelerate your brand effectiveness. Candidates are always looking at how much you are treating your different employees with dignity and respect regardless of their different backgrounds.

Now will move to the next step in the brand strategy and it is the brand execution.

Employment Brand Execution

At this stage you use what you have created in the previous stage in terms of the brand message creation as the cornerstone to execute your brand strategy which is mainly communicating the brand message. Brand Message Communication has two ways:

- Internal Brand Communication.
- External Brand Communication.

At the first one you use the outcome from your engagement survey to put your action plan to tackle the internal engagement problems. We mentioned that the key to an effective external brand is your inside working environment and how effective it is in satisfying the employee needs. Happy employees are the key to attract the needed talent. They are the ones who will talk positively about your organisation and thus encouraging the potential candidates to come and apply to your organisation.

Here I will focus on the importance of following up on your employees' engagement level continuously. The issue of the engagement is not a one-time survey you do every once in a while. It should be a key principle within your employee excellence programs. You should aspire to create a culture that is based on a mutual respect between the employees and the employer and to strive to motivate the employees to the degree that they are willing to go the extra mile for the company. This is called Employees Engagement.

HR professionals can use the following tips to support their internal brand execution:

1. To check in with the departments in their organisations regularly through pulse surveys to know if the engagement level is as requested to be.
2. To communicate heavily with the department heads about their expectation from their employees and how can HR support to create a

positive work experience that ultimately will support the brand image of the organisation.
3. Provide coaching for the department heads about how to provide the proper coaching and communication to their employees which will contribute to the brand execution effectiveness.

The second way is about communicating your brand message to the outside (External Brand Communication) is in summary about taking advantage of your internal brand strength and to convey these strengths to the potential candidates though multiple ways. You could use your website to publish your core values and what distinguishes you from others on the front page. Millennials are more prone than any other generation to explore organisation website before they apply to that organisation and they are attracted to how much the website is well designed or how much it is attractive.

You could also use other approaches to convey your brand message like the job fairs or by participating in charitable events as part of your corporate social responsibility which will have the biggest impact in the new generations entering the workforce.

The main issue here is not about how you convey your brand message but rather how genuine you are in your brand message. Is it really an authentic message that reflects your work environment? There are a lot of NGOs (non-governmental organisations) that don't do any promotion for their employment but they are well-recognised to the degree that a lot of people aspire to join such organisations. It's the cause that they pursue that make candidates attracted to such organisations.

Employment Brand Evaluation

Evaluating employment brand is not a straightforward process that has a defined set of metrics as per the other HR areas we have discussed in this book. But there are some aspects that we must put into consideration when we measure our brand effectiveness.

The first indicator through which you can measure your brand effectiveness is how much your organisation is considered an Employer of choice. In principle this is the most desirable outcome of the whole brand issue. Your goal is to make your organisation as an attraction force so that candidates are lured to apply to your organisation.

This area is measured through tracking the number of the candidates who applied to your organisation in a certain time period. But most importantly you need to correlate the number of candidates who applied to a certain vacancy with how much you were successful in converging these candidates into new hires. It's important to increase the bulk of the candidates who apply to your organisation but it's more important to measure who is really interested to join your organisation.

We mentioned before how vital it is to balance between your external brand identity and your internal work environment. By maintaining this balance, you can enhance the conversion rate of the potential candidates into successful hires.

The other measure that your brand effectiveness should impact positively is your **Recruitment Process Effectiveness**. By that I mean how smooth is the transition rate of the candidates from one stage in the recruitment process to another. The perception of the candidates who apply to a vacancy into your organisation about your brand effectiveness encourages them to move forward in the recruitment process. Your ultimate goal and measure of your recruitment effectiveness is the offer acceptance rate of the candidates throughout the recruitment process.

The final measure is your **Engagement Index**. We talked comprehensively about this issue and how to tackle it but here I will focus on the importance of tracking your **Turnover** rate as a key indicator of your engagement effectiveness. Again, if you are being effective in the first two measures of your brand (employer of choice and recruitment process effectiveness) but the turnover measure is not effective (high turnover) then there is a big issue with your employee engagement level.

Training and Development

Introduction

It has been said a lot that training and development are the key drivers to achieve the excellence in today's organisations. But unfortunately, not all the organisations are giving the needed importance and focus regarding their training function. There are many studies all over the world that show how many organisations have fallen apart because of not providing the proper training to their employees. These companies are always complaining that training is a costly expenditure that increases their financial burden which would ultimately affect their profit margins.

The problem begins from the perception of these organisations and how they approach their training departments or functions. As per the past paragraph these organisations consider training as an expenditure. This perception has been around for many years and it affected the well-being of the training professionals and the training departments alike. In the times of the recession the first thing these organisations mostly do is to cut their training budgets. Changing this negative perception about the training and development is our responsibility.

The inherent problem when it comes to the training and development is the measurement side of the function. There is a big difference between T&D and the other HR functions when it comes to the measurement side. All the other HR functions could survive without a clear measurement framework but it's the opposite when it comes to the training and development function. If you hired a qualified candidate without measuring the cost neither the time you spent filling the vacancy, the probability that the stakeholders in your organisation won't recognise your efforts is less likely to happen.

The level of the performance exerted from the new candidate and how she/he is demonstrating tangible performance is already evident and recognised from everyone. If you introduced a revised pay structure and the employees were very happy because their salaries have been adjusted then most probably you won't have to measure the satisfaction of your employees regarding their happiness from the new pay structure. The outcomes from both the recruitment and the compensation functions were to a big extent evident and clear without the need to a measurement framework.

But this is not to underestimate the role the HR analytics play in leveraging your HR function. The previous examples are only introduced in order to show the importance of the measurement of the T&D function. Now going back to the measurement of the T&D. If you introduced a new training program for your front-line customer reps and it was approved by your management and after the training has been completed you didn't attempt to measure if the training has accomplished its objectives. What do you think the result would be?

The participants in the training would be happy at first and the same situation applies to their managers but after few months you will notice a big resentment from both the trainees and their managers. The trainees are frustrated because they didn't have any opportunity to apply the knowledge and the skills they gained and their managers didn't see any performance improvement on the departmental level. This is the biggest challenge when not measuring the training return and how it impacted your organisation. No effect is apparent from your training programs unless you measure it first.

The lack of attention to the training function has contributed to a drastic skill gap universally. Organisations are always attributing this skill gap to the learning systems in the universities and how they fall short in preparing the new graduates to the labour market. It could be true that the learning systems in the universities all over the world are suffering from the lack of the integration with the market labour needs but I believe that the major problem is the lack of the proper training opportunities that the organisations should provide to their employees.

Most the organisations are not dealing with the training needs of their employees systematically as for the other HR domains. The conventional wisdom is that the day to day work experience will take care of the employees' competence but in fact this approach is not that much effective as when you plan for the training of your employees thoughtfully and deliberately. And even if it happened that some organisations are assigning training provisions in their yearly budgets the deployment of the training actions on a yearly basis is not consistent with the individual training needs.

I have witnessed in many cases how the training plan for many employees were cut due to emerging business demands that were considered a forcing priority more than the training itself. In other cases, other employees were sent to training events with no clear or direct link to their skill gaps. This dilemma has been a historical struggle for many organisations and that's why the modern HR departments are considering the onboarding programs a key component of their departments.

The onboarding programs are a strategic way to align your training budgets with the training and development needs of your new comers whether they were juniors or seniors. Onboarding take care of the employees' development actions during the first 12 to 18 months. After that comes the role of the performance management function and its contribution to long term employee's development plans.

Going back to the 4 levels of HR excellence model you can notice that the training and development and the performance management are both located in the same segment. Now we moved from the foundational HR level to the intermediate level toward more strategic HR areas. Again, all the foundational capabilities in the model are of utmost importance to the whole model that if not managed as should be then the implications on the above strategic levels are negative.

Due to the high level of overlap and integration between T&D and the performance management I thought at first to write about the two subjects under one section. When you talk about T&D alone you are for sure reaching at a disadvantage, your training plan without a consistent and effective performance management system will suffer from big shortcomings. The most evident shortcoming is a general training plan that is not focused on the real skill gaps of the employee.

On the other side an effective performance management system supported by a weak T&D function won't sustain the long-term results as you aspire to have. A training need assessment that is not competency based will yield untargeted training needs that will ultimately increase the learning time needed for the employees. These two functions are complimentary to each other but in order to make the understanding of these two functions easier I decided to write about them separately.

Training and Development Essentials

Competency-Based Training

The topic of the competency based training begins by defining what's the meaning of Competency. Competencies as I defined them before comprises KSAOs (knowledge, skills, abilities and other characteristics). As a reminder on the definition of competencies I will list the definition once again:

1. Knowledge: is the body of information you need to acquire for certain competency.
2. Skills: is the proficiency level in applying the knowledge.
3. Abilities: your ability to demonstrate the knowledge and the skills in a given situation successfully.
4. Other Characteristics: are the other traits and/or job requirements that are not core to the main competency but would complement it in certain areas (They don't fall under KSAs).

A lot of us when hearing the concept (competency-based training) think that the concept is about delivering training to your employees as per their individual training needs as an outcome of the performance review process. Usually it's true but if we examined the elements of the competency's definition more closely, we find that the concept extends the idea of delivering training to more other actions.

Training interventions mainly target the skill gaps for the employees as part of their job description. But what about the knowledge part? Do you have to take training to fill a knowledge gap? Of course not. You can instruct your employee to read specialised technical articles or technical operations manuals to fill that knowledge gap. You could also have the support of your managers to deliver on the job training to fill skills gap which means that skill gaps could be tackled without the need for a formal training program.

Another important support factor for both the knowledge and the skills is the coaching delivered from the managers. Without it there could be a risk that any organisation will lose any new gained knowledge and skills acquired through its employees. So, the issue of the competency-based training is more than delivering training courses. It's a comprehensive approach that touches a lot of things that span the employee life cycle.

After this comes identifying your targeted audience. The employees who will receive the proper kind of training intervention is of utmost importance in order to plan for a consistent competency-based approach. By that I mean to classify your employees into groups that have common training needs so you maximise your efforts and investment. The classification in this case is based on the employee level. Senior professionals who have common customer service competency gaps regardless of their job might be gathered and given specific customer service training courses that would enhance this weakness.

Identifying the competency standards and levels is also another crucial step when it comes to designing your competency-based training programs. Usually most training programs comes as an outcome of a generic competency standards assessment. So, if you are aiming to develop your salespeople sales competencies and your sales competencies are generic like if you said the following regarding the negotiation competency (To reach a mutual agreement with the customer that preserves both the company and the customers right) then the training action plan won't be targeted specifically to fix the salespeople sales skills gaps.

This statement is very general and rarely you can reach anywhere by relying on evaluating the sales people against this statement alone. But if you said the following (level one sales people agree quickly on a win-win solution, level two salespeople plan for a long-term strategy regarding the customers complaints in order to reach an agreement) the salespeople will be developed according to an action plan that deals with a specific training outcome.

Another determinant factor to guarantee that the outcomes of the competency assessment and the corresponding training are deployed successfully is the immediate implementation of the training taken by the employee. All the previous work is not of big value unless you plan from the beginning how to make sure that the training that took place has been put into action. This aspect is related directly to the effectiveness of your training evaluation which will be discussed later on in this chapter. The purpose of the competency-based training is to build certain competency so what's the benefit of designing an effective competency-based training that doesn't translate into concrete action plan in the practical side of the work life.

Competency verification is also a very important point in the competency-based training compliance issue (as I like to call it) and it's related to the previous step. Here the HR professional must follow up closely on the ground the extent to which the competency-based training results have contributed to the development of the people who went through the whole process. As mentioned before it's important to guarantee that the training has taken place in the day-to-day business life of the employee but is it enough just to check the box that the training was implemented? Someone could say that it's more than enough to have that side of the competency-based training to guarantee a successful outcome.

In my opinion it's more complicated than that. What if a training program was aimed to develop the planning and organising competency but on the ground the program has done less than expected regarding the competency level of the people who went through the program although they were enthusiastic to apply it in their jobs and a big deal of the implementation has taken place. One of the biggest mistakes that happens during the training design stage is the inconsistency between the assessment and the design stages.

You can find that there is a lot of accuracy and information available during the assessment stage but the problem lies in how to create a vital link between the assessment results and the design stage. Let's suppose that the assessment stage regarding the planning and organising training has shown that the majority of the trainees who went through the assessment have a problem in allocating additional resources to guarantee a successful completion of their pending projects but the training has tackled the planning and organising competency with a big focus on how to prioritise tasks and a less focus on the resource allocation area.

In such a case the outcome of the training was not so effective because the major weakness wasn't tackled comprehensively. To avoid this mistake, we must design the training program according to the assessment outcomes. Unfortunately, in reality this matter is very difficult to attain due to many reasons. First of all, the training offerings in the majority of the training centres provide general training solutions that don't satisfy the competency gaps as per the level of the details we have just mentioned.

Not all the organisations also can afford to dedicate separate training functions that work closely with the department heads in order to design proper and detailed training plans which complicate the whole issue. Also, if the previous problems were resolved, there remains the major issue of designing a valid assessment tool that can elicit the right information needed to build on for the design stage.

All these problems make it very important to have a robust action plan in order to guarantee that our competency-based training programs are related to our employee's weakness in a detailed and specific manner that deals with their specific competency needs.

Lastly but not least is the metrics you set for the training programs that you design. Metrics are the performance standards that you assign per each competency in order to make sure that the training-based competency has reached its goals. Again, metrics and measurement of the training will be discussed later on but here I will just highlight on the importance of assigning related metrics that take into consideration the expected behaviours that the training must yield. By doing that you can guarantee that your competency-based training programs are reviewed continually and are up to date in terms of their content validity and relatedness to your workforce needs.

Leadership Competency-Based Development

John Maxwell has said that "Everything rises and falls on leadership." Indeed, this so true. I have personally witnessed the demise of many departments and companies because of the leadership styles prevailing in these organisations. Of course, leadership is more than using the proper leadership style, it comprises many other important qualities and behaviours. Leadership requires leaders to lead by example, to do what they preach. Leadership requires a genuine interest in the people whom you are leading, to take care of them and to solve their problems once they arise without any delay.

Leadership has been a major interest of many business authors and researchers for many decades because the subject in itself is luring enough to attract any person who has a passion to make a difference whether it is in business or in the personal life. In this book I will not talk about leadership as a distinctive topic, rather I will talk about how important it is for HR to dedicate the resources and attention to develop leadership capabilities for your company's leaders. Leaders (differentiated from managers) are the key to achieve the success of any organisation. Without them no organisation can sustain its success.

In many researches it was evident that a lot of organisations that celebrated years of success followed by long periods of downturn had mediocre leadership potential and effectiveness. Organisations that can sustain consistent and prosperous outcomes for the long run are the ones that have extraordinary leadership potential within their organisational layers. Leadership is a make or break factor in any organisation so HR professionals must pay attention to their leaders and they must occupy a big portion of their plans.

The other side is the HR leaders themselves and their leadership potential. Without the prudent leadership no HR person regardless of his/her leadership competence or the technical HR knowledge he/she has can achieve the HR excellence and the success aspired. Our work as an HR professional is very distinctive; it stems out from the HR department boundaries but it is reflected on and touches the overall organisational performance on the contrary from the rest of the departments, their work stems out from their boundaries but it is reflected on and touches their performance.

This principle is very important to understand and to digest. In order to understand more what do we mean by that let's look at the following example. Let's suppose that you are designing an onboarding program that will help to enhance the retention rate of your organisation. Who is the most beneficiary of this program? It's of course the head of departments who are in need to retain their newly talented hires. But if the sales department has introduced a new sales strategy that helped to leverage the organisational sales volumes and profits then who is the most beneficiary of that strategy. Of course they are the salespeople who will reap more cash rewards as a result of the new sales.

You need here just to notice that I said the most beneficiary which means that there are other stakeholders who will benefit from these developments. In the case of the onboarding program the HR manager would benefit also from the new onboarding program but the impact of this program would be low for HR if we compared it with the overall impact on the other departments in the organisation. In the case of the sales strategy that increased the sales volume the whole organisation would benefit also from the program at least in terms of the financial stability that means more employment stability but again the sales department would reap the direct benefits in terms of having more financial rewards.

The aforementioned instils the ideas that all what we do as HR professionals must have two elements:

1. All our strategies, programs and actions must be designed with a customer service approach, which means that these actions are all geared for the benefit of the organisational stakeholders.
2. HR must exhibit the needed leadership behaviours during these times in order to guarantee that the outcome of these programs is positively impacting the whole organisation with a big focus on developing the leadership potential of the line managers.

When the HR managers are able to achieve the leadership excellence for both themselves and the line managers then the organisation is definitely moving toward the right track.

In order to achieve the leadership excellence for your leaders and leadership potential you must pursue the following path:

1. To identify a specific competency framework for your leaders that is based on the business needs. This competency should be one of the major outcomes of the leaders' vision in the organisation. If for example the leadership in your organisation is seeking to expand its regional network into a global one then you need to embed the global and cultural effectiveness as one of your leadership competencies. Usually what most organisations do is to select one of the common leadership competency models available in the market and to use them as measurement tool. This approach cold work at the beginning as a starting point but it won't serve you in the long run. It could help you to establish for the culture of continuous learning you aspire to have but it can't move you to a new strategic performance level. That's why I emphasise again how important it is to design a leadership competency framework that is aligned with your strategies.
2. The next step is to design a valid measurement tool for the competency framework you have designed. But before that you need to identify the competency standards for each competency. These performance standards are a key way to base the mangers' assessment against a solid and valid criterion. It also helps the managers to be as objective as possible. A related example would be the following, you mention under the strategic management area that your managers are required to excel at the strategic management competency through attaining the following knowledge, skills and abilities:

- Demonstrating an advance knowledge level in the industry trends.
- Highly skilled in strategic analysis tools like SWOT and PESTLE.
- Ability to deal with and react to sudden setbacks and market volatility with positive attitude.

Then comes your role to design the appropriate measurement tool. My advice to you is not to waste your time trying to create this measurement tool if you don't have the appropriate expertise to do so. You have two choices to solve this problem, you can have the help of an outside consultant who can help you to design the measurement tool or if your budget doesn't allow you to do that, you can purchase off-the-shelf leadership competency measurement tool that would save you the time and money. But you need to be careful in your selection as to selecting a tool that is far away from the needed competencies you want to measure.

3. After that comes the important step of making the actual assessment for your leaders. Within this context I recommend to use a multi-rater assessment approach because it generates a more valid and comprehensive data than if you followed only a single individual assessment. An important tip for you here is to make the leaders aware of the consequences of that assessment. Usually when we hear the word consequences, we think that there will be a negative effect on the leaders who don't attain an acceptable evaluation rate but it's contrary to that. We mean to tell the leaders in advance that the outcome of this assessment is meant to leverage the leaders' capabilities and competence to the level that the business would thrive and that with the company supporting them they are required to go the extra mile in order to achieve the optimal results that would benefit them and the organisation alike.

4. The action (learning) plan. This is the most important element in the whole process, here you make sure that the outcome of the previous three steps is put into action in order to guarantee that the leaders are changing their behaviours as requested by their senior management. The action plan would be a blended approach of self-learning courses, instructor-led training courses, coaching and on-the-job training. The most important thing is to integrate these elements into the performance action plan for the senior managers or else you will jeopardise your overall leadership excellence level in the organisation. Within the performance action plan, you must identify the KPIs that are linked with achieving the performance goals. Here you will need to plan for three tiers of the managerial KPIs, short-term, medium-term and long-term KPIs. At every level you should assign a portion of the performance goals that are achievable and that are leveraged into higher calibre once you finish every level and when you are approaching a higher one. I will give the example of a new appointed HR manager in Alpha company who is assigned the goal of implementing a performance management system in the company. The three tier KPIs model is demonstrated in the below pyramid.

Figure 25 – The Three Tier KPIs Model: Performance Management System Example

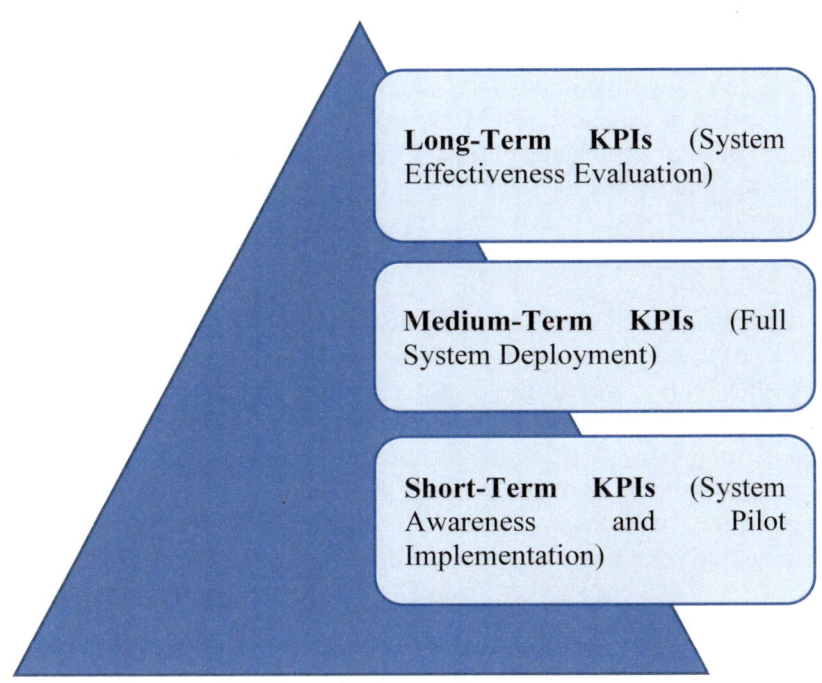

As you can notice from the above graph that the HR manager in this example is demanded to achieve their KPIs on three levels. The first one is the short-term KPIs and in this case the performance management system awareness between the organisational stakeholders and the pilot implementation are crucial for the overall system's success. You can't here assign the full system implementation as a KPI at the first level because rationally it's nearly impossible to deploy a complicated system like the performance management from the first time or within a one-year timeframe and to expect that it will succeed.

Such a KPI is mostly applicable and affordable to be achieved after the first tier KPI as the HR manager had the time to navigate through the system complexity and accordingly, she was able to deploy the system on a wider scale. The last tier KPI and which is the system effectiveness evaluation by default has been assigned the top of the pyramid as a natural step that comes after the first two tiers. This methodology should be applicable with all the managerial and leadership levels and roles if you were to guarantee a successful learning plan implementation as part of the leadership competency-based development.

5. The action plan effectiveness evaluation. This is the final step in the leadership competency-based development process. You need here to establish the measurement framework that will enable you to decide whether your investment into your leadership development programs has brought the agreed upon benefits. The KPIs you have identified in

the previous step will guide you through this evaluation process. Related to our previous example and if we were at the second tier KPI (performance management full system deployment) then this KPI should be translated into related actions that will prove the outcome whether it was negative or positive. In this case particularly you can use the BSCM (Balanced Scorecard Model) as your framework in order to measure how effective you were in applying this system. The BSCM would be reflected into a survey through which you probe the system effectiveness (the BSCM as reflected on performance management will be discussed in more details in the next chapter).

The aforementioned steps (the leadership competency-based development framework) are only one part of the leadership comprehensive development plans that many organisations use. Some organisations might use the global assignment as a support framework for their leadership development plans. Others might use executive coaching. Whatever the process is, the most important point is that you leaders are a make or break factor in the whole organisational excellence process and thus paying close attention to that issue is no longer an option, it's a must in order to survive in today's business world. In addition to that your success as an HR professional is dependent heavily on the organisational leaders' success.

HR-Led Learning Is a Success Factor

Historically training as a function has been undermined. The main reason behind that notion was the decentralisation of the training function and its administration. But why the decentralisation of the training is a problem? Isn't it (Decentralisation) a good recipe for success whether it was for the training or any other decision-making authority? In principle decentralisation in many aspects was an effective solution for many business challenges but when it comes to training the issue is totally different.

What has been done is that the head of departments were used to provide their training needs to their direct managers and they in their turn would approve it and then the training would take place. Form here started the problem of training underappreciation. The HODs care about getting their people to the training rooms only. They believe that the training delivery and its supposed consequences of knowledge and skills transfer to their organisations is the sole responsibility of the trainer or the coach.

In some part, it's true when it comes to the motivation side of the participants and how to make them eager to apply what they have learned, the issue gets more complicated. But is it enough to rely on the trainer only to cover that crucial part which is the training implementation in the workplace? Of course, it isn't. HR has the ultimate responsibility of managing the training function and to guarantee that the training will take place when the trainees get back to their offices. Form here started the revolution of the training modern management. A milestone in the training literature is Donald Kirkpatrick's book (Evaluating Training Programs).

Through this book he introduced the idea of measuring the effectiveness of any training program you give to your employees. He designed a four levels methodology that any organisation can use in order to measure how effective the training was in delivering its outcomes. These levels are the reaction, learning, transfer to the job and the results level. Kirkpatrick has emphasised the importance of the third level as a key driver to transfer the learning or the behaviour change that happened to the workplace. He reinforced that a make or break element in this area is the direct manager and how he/she is supporting the transfer of the knowledge or the new behaviours to the workplace.

But the issue of the learning transfer won't be completely successful even if the direct manager was supportive for that process. HR must have the upper hand in managing and directing the whole process. And to be more specific the training function must be centralised in HR. within this context HR shouldn't have a complete centralisation of the function or else the participative approach with the head of the departments will be damaged. HR people must help the HODs throughout the training process starting from the needs assessment through the training evaluation. The benefits of centralising the function are to help attribute the training outcome to the HR's efforts.

HR must be held accountable when it comes to measuring the training effectiveness. The department heads are not alone in the process and by relying on them solely you are jeopardising the training effectiveness in your organisation. The process of the training delivery and how to take advantage of the training outcomes has been a struggle for many companies for long periods. Companies invest big amounts of dollars annually in the training function but the return is nearly diminished, the problem again is not the training itself or the participants who took the training. The problem is much bigger than that. It's the issue of identifying what's really needed in terms of the skill gaps. And the most important thing is how to link these needs with the overall organisational strategy.

If HR is really a business partner then he/she will have the advance knowledge about the direction the company is targeting and accordingly the issue of designing the training strategy will be much easier. I mentioned before how I worked with the HR and the training team in Jordan Tractor company on minimising the training period of the technicians from three to one year. This accelerated training program didn't come by coincidence, in fact it was a reflection of the senior management's strategy of taking advantage of the business potential of the mining sector in Jordan.

Advancing the service side of the process through the service department was a vital issue. it was important to increase the number of machines sold for the mining customers but what was more important is to provide a long-term support for these customers by offering them the needed maintenance and repairs. At that time, we didn't have the needed workforce capability in terms of the numbers and the quality and the fact that the miming business was booming rapidly in a fast pace more than we expected didn't leave us any long-term options, even the mid-terms strategies to recap on that expansion was not an option.

So, we began our strategy on recruiting the needed numbers of the technicians both the experienced and the newly graduates. It was much easier to select from the diploma graduates who provided us with a big pool of candidates. These graduates were young and full of energy and the quality of learning they got through the learning systems they went through was much higher and better than the old learning systems decades ago. We have made on-campus recruitment for many colleges all over the country until we found the candidates whom we believed will add value and will help to achieve the organisational goals for the future.

After we have went through a long and exhausting period of recruiting and selecting the right candidates and after they have joined the organisation, we began the deployment of the accelerated training program for these technicians. A lot of deliberate efforts were put to reach to the point where a condensed training program (mainly narrowed down from three to one year) would yield the same value as for the original lengthy training program. The end result was astonishing after the first year, we had really brilliant technicians who were able to do the basic maintenance work in a very accurate and proficient way.

What I wanted to convey is the following, the HR department was able to make a strategic transition in the way how things were run out before, especially for the training function which has struggled a lot historically. This major change was not possible if HR was not on top of the organisational business awareness. Also, the centralisation of the training function within the HR boundaries was a crucial factor in boosting the whole process. This is the meaning of having an HR-lead training function that can contribute effectively to the overall goals of the organisation.

By rooting the training function as a major HR function that is led and managed by HR you can guarantee that your ROI of your training programs is very high and you can contribute in turn to the overall success of your organisation.

Creating A Culture of Learning

Before I begin with this topic, I want to highlight again on the concept of culture that we previewed previously in this book. The definition is the following *Culture is the repetitive routines and behaviours that happen continuously and deliberately forming the organisation's collective identity that it becomes nearly impossible to change its components.* This concept is very important to digest and understand in order to know how to move into creating new and innovative ways that make it easy to create the culture of learning that you aspire to have.

The most important part of the concept that I will highlight on is (that it becomes nearly impossible to change its components) the one that seems odd if we analysed the whole concept and broke it down to its elements. I will not bother you in analysing the first part (the repetitive routines and behaviours that happen continuously and deliberately forming the organisation's collective identity) because it's obvious and easy to understand. The problem lies with the second one. It might seem that the concepts imply that a culture will never change.

It's not true as cultures change holistically in the way the individuals do their work and how they interact with each other. The thing that is nearly impossible to change is the people who drive the culture. In more specific terms I am talking here about the psychology of the people in any organisation. People who are introverted or the people who are driven by numbers and analytics as an example have internal tendency to do so, this is the aspect of the people that is nearly impossible to change.

The other aspect that is easily changeable if tackled with the right intervention are the behaviours that people exhibit on a daily basis. If you came to a new organisation as an HR director and you found most of the employees in the organisation including yours are not approaching their managers when facing a new problem into their daily work life then this could be changed because mostly it's not related to the psychology of the employees. The reason could be that the trust level between the employees and their managers has been bad historically for many reasons.

All what you need to do is to find strategies and actions that will bridge the gap between the employees and their managers. You could do for example a team building events designed by an external consultant and to deploy it on a departmental level through which you gather the department head and their employees for several days in order to facilitate a new trust level and thus rooting the new positive relationship that will help achieve your goals. The same thing applies to creating a culture of learning.

Employees are always eager to get the training they need whether it was on the job (mostly delivered by a mentor or a coach) or through a third party specialised in the training delivery. The major problem when it comes to creating a culture of learning is twofold. The first one is the employees themselves. Here I'm talking about the resistance you could find when you are trying to disseminate new concepts in the workplace. So, we will agree first that learning is not confined by training delivery only.

Learning could be dealing with new ways in how you approach your job (e.g. give training to your HR team on how to do job analysis in a new and modified way) or it could be deploying a BYOD (bring your own device) policy which requires changing the whole way how employees interact with their daily tasks and their colleagues within a new context that governs this relationship. Employees resistance is represented mainly by a big desire to stay where they are today and a bigger desire not to move to a new status to or change their current way of doing things. The resistance in the case of deploying a new process or system is usually higher than that of applying new skills gained through traditional training methods.

In the first case the employees don't have that much control on the process they are trying to adapt with or to implement, there are factors that are out of their control that if not taken care of could easily destroy and attempt to a new change initiative. If the employee is part of a team project that aims to enhance the production line of its factory and this project is interdependent with more than one project then she could face some problems like not having the needed help from other teams to complete the project.

When it comes to applying new skills that the employee has gained when attending training program then it could be much easier to apply the skills because the employee has a big control over the element of his/her job and thus the process of converting the skills into the job is achievable to a great extent. Of course, if the employee has faced a block from their manager that prevented them from applying the new skills then it could hamper the whole thing.

The resistance from the employees when it comes to making a change is a natural response that we must expect, even more we must be sure that it's coming. HR professionals who underestimate this important aspect or don't deal with it seriously when it comes to the surface are definitely going to face big problems that could jeopardise their change initiatives. If we accepted that the employee resistance is part of any change initiative then our lives are going to become easier because we accounted for that reaction before we started so dealing with it when it's accounted and planned for will make a big difference in terms of the output we aspire to achieve.

But how we can overcome that resistance? As we said it can be managed and mitigated through a deliberate and thoughtful approach of dealing with it. Here I will highlight on John Kotter change management model that he introduced in his book *Leading Change*. Specifically, I will highlight on the first four stages in his model and they are:

- Establish a sense of urgency.
- Create a guiding coalition.
- Develop a vision and strategy.
- Communicate the change vision.[2]

These steps are of paramount importance when we tackle new change initiatives or processes. It helps you to diagnose your current situation and the people underlying the change in order to be effective as much as possible when it comes to applying these changes. These four steps correspond to Kurt Lewin's change model's first step (Unfreeze). Here your role as an HR professional is to examine the psychological state of the employee going through the change and to find the best root possible in order to facilitate the change with the minimal resources and effort possible.

Developing a sense of urgency when it comes to learning could be achieved easily if you have the proper support system in place. In this case I am talking about the performance management system that should provide you and your organisation with any red alarms that could create a sense of urgency. It could

---

[2] John P. Kotter. Leading Change, 1996. The Eight-Stage Process.

be that the operation department is not responding to the customers' orders in due time because of an alarming performance gap.

To create a guiding coalition is made possible also when you partner with the department mangers as your major allies to your strategy when making learning a company-wide scale habit. Here you need to find a proper way to overcome the resistance of these managers which is the second important resistance factor you will face after their employees. The success factor here is not the effort you exert trying to convince them of your change initiative but rather you need here to rely on the efforts you made long time before that in terms of the good relations and the trust you have built with these managers.

The other two steps (develop a vision and strategy & Communicate the change vision) are easily executed if you managed to be successful at the first two points. The four steps on Kotter's model are very good to follow if you want to create a culture of learning which is one of the biggest change initiatives any HR person could ever face. It could even work for any other change initiative you might go through.

Creating a culture of learning has become the norm in our competitive business world. If any company wants to sustain its existence in a very volatile world then learning is a key component of the overall strategy of any company. If you want to have a resilient organisation then you must have resilient employees who can deal with uncertainty with a high confidence level and equipped with the needed knowledge to beat that uncertainty. Continuous learning is the ultimate solution to create a resilient workforce.

Selecting Training Programs

I highlighted in some occasions during this book that I purposely excluded the theoretical framework of many HR functions that I have covered in this book. Again, my purpose was to refocus the reader's attention on the vital elements that if followed carefully then the results are going to be exemplary. One of the most well-known models in the training domain is the ADDIE (asses, design, develop, implement and evaluate) model which covers the training cycle from the beginning till the end.

Instead of writing about this model which you can find a lot of literature written about it I focused on a much more important issue related to the training effectiveness. I will introduce a question here for you to reflect on. Which is the factor that could lead to a successful training function in your organisation? Is it applying the ADDIE model as written in the HR books to find later that the employees in your organisation are not following through their learning plans? Or is it better to facilitate the concepts behind the new training methodology you follow and to manage the resulted resistance?

If you answered the question as I expect to then you will know why I didn't write about the theoretical part of the training and the same thing applies to all the functions covered within this book. The issue of selecting the proper training programs might seem easy when you look at it merely without deep investigation of the proper training courses that best fit the person and the company. Most of the mistakes that happen when it comes to selecting training programs is because of not relating the content of the training topics to the competency gaps of the employee.

In the next chapter we will see how much vital it is to link the outputs of the performance management system with the training and development function. In other words, the outputs of performance management are the inputs of the training and development function. Most of the training programs I have seen tackles the competency gaps in certain topic in a general way without paying attention to the specific needs of the employee. The extent to which the employees get benefit of any training program is related directly to how much the training was successful in solving a real-life problem that the employee is facing because of a competency gap.

In order to illustrate this, I will give the following example, let's suppose that you have a customer service department in a company that provides financial services for its clients. The nature of the customer service department work is different than the traditional ones. In this company the customer service representatives are required to go deep in certain issues with the customers. To send these employees to a traditional customer service training course that tackles the etiquette side of serving customers won't bring any benefit.

The nature of this company requires the customer service reps to have advance negotiation and persuasion skills to be presented in certain situations so here comes the need to examine carefully the content of that training course in order to have more targeted training approach that aims to tackle the competency gaps.

This aspect of the training administration side is very important to focus on if you want to have an effective outcome of your training programs. Companies invest big amounts of money on training its employees, but unfortunately the problems of the training administration including choosing the right training course that brings both related content to your need and effective outcome hinders a lot the training effectiveness. That's why you need to balance the matter of choosing the most cost-effective training course that has the right fit with your training needs.

There are some guidelines you can follow when you want to choose the right training course:

- The first important thing to do is to identify the competency gaps through a valid evaluation tool. If you don't have such tools then you need to rely on making a one-on-one session with the department manager and the employees whom you want to engage in this project. You need to gather qualitative information through which you can generate a survey or questionnaire to use as your reference evaluation tool.
- Before you begin sending request to the training companies for covering your training need it's advisable that you contact HR people in similar

companies if applicable in order to benchmark with them about similar experiences that they might have went through.
- After choosing the training companies that you have identified as potential ones you can extend your efforts to attend a portion of similar training courses that the training company is delivering to other clients. This would give you an advantage to know about the proficiency level of the trainers of these training companies.
- Also, one of the recommendations that are of big value to your endeavour is to make one-on-one meetings between the trainer and the employees who will take the training, this would help you to gather more information about the validity of the training course to your training needs.

Measuring Training and Development Effectiveness

Now we are at the second level of measuring the HR excellence. Again, the measurement model here works in sequence, which means that every level whether we were exploring the knowledge part of it or the critical success factors that comprise it or whether we were talking about the measurement side of it the different levels build on each other's. You could be doing great achievement in the employment brand side of the model and thus creating a big pool of talent but your efforts in the training and development area is so weak that you can't retain such talent for the long run.

So, it doesn't make sense to begin measuring the training efforts you are doing before beginning the logical step of bringing talent to your organisation (And measuring your brand effectiveness) that can add value through the training and development programs you are offering. There are many companies that have a higher level of achievement in the training function although their brand efforts are weak and are not generating the needed talent nor retaining their current talent.

Someone could argue that your effectiveness in the first one (the T&D management) is not dependent nor is it affected by the second one (the brand management). Indeed, they are. It doesn't affect you as an organisation if there are some shortcomings in the brand segment but overall you're doing so well in the training and development function. You are developing the skills of the current staff and by doing that you are working on retaining them. Again, it could be true. This issue holds two important issues, the first one is the talent pipeline you should be maintaining and the second one is the complimentary side of the employment brand (The engagement level of the employee).

Your weakness as an employer of choice for the outside candidates could put you in a risky situation in terms of the number of the candidates who are interested to join you. The danger is more than that, it extends to your employees also, they are in their turn wouldn't be tempted nor interested to stay with you on the long run. If your brand is not marketable in your region, then your employee will look for sure for an employer who is more popular and whom they can add their name on their resume proudly.

Whether we liked it or not, the candidates and the employees in any organisation are both interested in a robust brand that can add to their career journey. The historical employer-employee relationship which was based on a mutual commitment from both sides and which resulted in a long-term employment or even in the cases where it resulted in a lifetime employment has gone away. Now the candidates are looking to be employed by a famous employer that they can brag about and once they have found their next target; they will move with no hesitation.

The second important thing that reemphasises the importance of the sequence of the measurement model and as related to our example is the engagement level of your employees. Focusing in our example on training your employees without any related link with the brand effectiveness means that you are developing your employees without paying attention to their most important issue, which is that the engagement, training and development on its own is not enough to attract and most importantly to retain your top talent. In fact, most of the time you train your employees to find that they will leave you once they land a new attractive job. This example was important as an illustration on the importance of going into a sequential mode when it comes to the HR excellence model and its measurement.

The issue of measuring training effectiveness is not normal or easy to conceptualise as for the other functions in our model in this book. The major issue here that prevented me from writing comprehensively about measuring the training and development function is Donald Kirkpatrick's model in measuring training effectiveness. His model is a milestone in this area and writing anything else other than that model is a not so effective and will not bring us any added value on how to measure the training effectiveness.

But for the purpose of narrowing the gap between the management side of the training and its measurement I will write about the training measurement from two perspectives; the first one is the operational side of the training measurement and the second one is the strategic part. The strategic part deals with Kirkpatrick's methodology, and within the context of this book I will highlight on this model briefly just for you to have an idea about how the model works in action. I'll leave the rest for you to discover this model in more detail by referring to one of Kirkpatrick's books about the model.

The operational side of the training measurement as I see it includes four major metrics:

1. Training hours per employee.
2. Training cost per employee.
3. Training cost to HR cost.
4. T&D ROI (Return on Investment).

Training Hours Per Employee

This metric as for the rest of the other metrics falls under the operational side of the training measurement. By this I don't mean tracking your operational side of the training. Managing the training function operationally requires the day-to-day follow up on the training matters in addition to going through the complexity of the systematic ADDIE model that I mentioned earlier.

Operational within this context means that the metrics used here are indicative of the strategic side of the function. This metric (Training hours per employees) that we are discussing is the outcome of the following formula, the **training hours per employees delivered in a timeframe divided by the numbers of employees who attended the training.** It's easily calculated and doesn't need a lot of effort to gather or to analyse its information.

The value of this metric lies behind a deeper analysis beyond the metric itself. let's say that you were tracking the training hours for your employees during the last three years. In the first two years you achieved your target as an organisation by delivering 60 hours of training per each employee which was your target. The third year was a turnaround because of a bad financial performance of your company which affected negatively the number of training hours delivered.

The result was a decrease in the total training hours delivered to the half. When we look at this metric over three years period the first impression we get is that the performance of the company should be better in the first two years because the number of the training hours delivered to the employee hit the target while it should be worse in the third year because of the decrease in the training hours.

This premise is not actually true if we gathered more information on the effect of the training delivered to the employees by using the Kirkpatrick model. Reaching to the third and fourth levels of the model you discover that the new behaviours the employees have gained were not delivered successfully on the job in the first two years and in turn the impact on the business was not effective.

In the third year although the training hours were cut to the half you discovered that the effect of the training related to the same two levels of Kirkpatrick's model were much better than the first two years. How this could happen? There are many reasons behind this. The managers for some departments in the third year have excreted extra efforts to help their employees to apply what they have learned on the job which resulted in a better organisational performance.

So, following through this metrics merely without going further into the process of discovering more information behind the metric won't reveal much for you. In the previous example the effectiveness of the training on the company level was not related directly to the number of the training hours only, there were other factors that helped to enhance the organisational effectiveness.

This metric is the baseline for you as an HR professional in order to build a valid case of whether the training has achieved its goals or not but don't rely on it solely as it would not help you just to track the number of hours. It's about the quality of your approach, not the quantity you achieve.

Training Cost Per Employee

The formula of this metric is calculated by dividing the **training cost by the total number of employees.** Again, the calculation of this metric is easy but like the previous metric it serves as a baseline to start from in order to build a more strategic training and development function. Here we must relate this metric with two sides, the first one is the fourth level of Kirkpatrick's model (The results) and the second one is the ROI (Return on investment).

The fourth level of Kirkpatrick's model deals with the effect of the training on the overall performance of the company. Knowing the cost of the training you gave to your employees during a year timeframe will help you to do the cost and return calculations that we will just see in the final metric, it also gives you a track tool to know if the training budget is being allocated properly all over the year.

Many companies define a training annual budget but they don't stick to it. They sometimes deviate from the assigned amount of investment allocated for certain departments resulting in negative deviation, like if the sales department T&D budget was 25000 USD and you invested 32000 USD. The reason could be a misjudgement the year before on the training cost and most importantly it could be a performance management related issue.

If your performance management system doesn't help you to identify the real areas of improvement for your employees in the sales department in our last example then the estimation of the needed budget for the next year is not going to be accurate. An example of this would be that the KPIs (Key Performance Indicators) are not accurately measuring the needed performance of your sales people. They were focusing on capturing the outcomes of the sales department performance (the money side) rather than focusing on the way how they achieved their target.

The bottom line is the following, although this metric and the one before (Training Hours Per Employee) are transactional in their nature but they impose an important strategic side of measuring the training function effectiveness if they were put into broader context as I've just explained.

Training Cost to HR Cost

This metric is calculated by dividing the training cost by HR cost. This metric is complimentary to the previous metric and it serves the purpose of examining your budget allocation regarding the training and development function. It also helps you to identify if the spending on your training as part of your HR budget is appropriate. Appropriate here means that the proportion of the HR spending on T&D is fair and covers the whole workforce training requirements.

Here there is a very important element that we should look at. If the training function is centralised into the HR function then the cost tracking and allocation on the training function is managed easily. If the training function is spread over the departments in the organisation then the cost management and allocation is difficult. It easy for you as an HR professional to determine if a training topic is relevant to your workforce needs if you have the call on deciding on the training rather than receiving an order from a department manager on a training topic she assigned to her team.

I have faced similar situations many times. I saw a lot of training dollars being spent on many training topics that were not relevant to the organisational realities. I remember when a sales manager in a company I worked for convinced the general manager to spend money on a data analytics training thinking that the trainees would be able to help the company better if they worked through a data analytics approach.

I told the manager that our team is not ready yet for such a move. The data in our company were not captured easily, it was fragmented in many stand-alone systems, the managers in our company were not accustomed to data analytics field. They hadn't practiced it before. The most important thing is that they didn't realise that building analytics excellence requires patience. You need to build few years of databases through which you can build a trend that will help you to take decisions. Having a centralised training function through HR is key to a successful training investment.

T&D ROI (Return On Investment)

This metric is very important and serves as the baseline from which you can judge whether or not to pursue a training intuitive or not. The formula of this metric is the following:

(Financial value of training initiative / cost of training initiative) × 100

The calculation of this metric gets harder when you pursue a training that doesn't corresponds to a profit and loss considerations like the soft skills training which is hard to relate to a quantifiable outcome.

For example, if you are planning for coaching skills training for your department managers as part of your performance management system deployment and you want to calculate the ROI you will find that its dynamics are numerous and will lead you to confusion on how to reach a satisfactory outcome that will help justify the training.

You need here (the scope explained here is not completely representative of a real-life situation) to show how much that training will contribute to enhancing the coaching skills of the manager as related to more engagement and better moral from the employees. Someone could say that linking coaching to engagement and morale only won't prove its effectiveness, you must extend your ROI calculation beyond that.

You need for example to show the correlation between the enhanced coaching skills and a better performance of the employees on the ground. Maybe you will correlate the skill enhancement with a lower turnover, a third justification could be to show how the coaching in the past helped to prepare the current generation of leaders who are steering the company.

As you can see that this justification requires a lot of effort and time in order to reach a rational outcome through which you can convince your management that the investment in certain training areas is required.

The issue of justifying the training return becomes easier when you are delivering training that corresponds to a more measurable outcome. If you are planning for a negotiation skills training for your salespeople then you can correlate the training outcomes with the increase in the sales figures. So, you can tell your management that the sales figure will increase in a certain percentage if the negotiation skills of the salespeople were enhanced.

You need here to link this justification with past similar cases if you have one. If not, you need to rely on a well trusted source or benchmark that will support your story. You could say that certain companies that have applied this training have witnessed an extraordinary increase in the sales figures. Both cases you are making a business case that will make your life easier when it comes to justifying training dollars.

I will preview a case that happened with me and it's a proof that ROI is a very important metric when it comes to justifying the training investment or not. I remember when the training supervisor who was reporting to me in a company that I worked for was enthusiastic to build a training centre with state-of-the-art tools and equipment. The goal was to train heavy equipment technician on the basic maintenance principles.

The idea was great as we were experiencing a big shortage in the needed numbers of the qualified technicians and the idea to attract talent form community colleges was a great move toward bridging the workforce gap that we had in this company. But here comes the key question, does it make a valid business case to build a training centre that will cost 125000 USD just to see a slight decrease in the number of redoes (to repeat a repair again due to its failure) per year?

This is the same question that I asked the training supervisor about. When we reflected on that question and gathered the needed data to answer it, we figured out that the percentage of redoes that we can decrease because of the training centre will have a financial effect of no more than 10000 USD per year. This opened our eyes on a very important fact that the training centre is not of big value and the expected return won't cover the amount if investment before ten years at least.

This simple calculation made us think in a new approach that would benefit us and at the same time would convince the management. Our solution was to adopt a trainer concept where the senior technician would occupy the role of a coach or a trainer and the junior technician would be the coaches. The investment for this solution was ten times less than the original investment proposed by the training supervisor and it was much more effective.

So, the bottom line was that a training proposal including all the details accompanied by the training like building a training centre would be much valid and convincing when you really highlight on the most effective way that is satisfactory and cost-effective at the same time for both the senior management and the department heads.

Kirkpatrick's Model

This model is the related to the strategic side of the training measurement topic. The aforementioned metrics as I stated before are operational in their nature unless you put them in a broader context. Kirkpatrick's model has been a lighthouse for many years and it's common and usable in many contexts in any kind of training in any place.

As I mentioned before that this model is very comprehensive to the degree that writing about it fairly in this book would create a confusion for the reader. My purpose in this book was clear from the beginning. I am writing about the critical success factors for any HR department in a way that is not so detailed and comprehensive.

My writing for this book was based on giving the reader what he or she needs to know about the major HR functions and to focus on really what makes a difference in the HR department. The rest of the process should be an individual effort form each one of you on how to search and probe the nuances of a certain topic. No one book on earth could answer all of your questions, you need to search for information beyond this book if you want to be an expert.

The goal of my book was to provide the reader with a framework that anyone can build upon. Believe me when I say to you that my journey through the past eight years to deploy this model was so exhausting. I needed a lot of personal effort in order to build my knowledge base and the competency needed in many aspects of the HR domain.

I made a lot of research and read many books on many different HR topics in order to support the deployment of this book. But all that effort was channelled in a systematic and methodical way. It was part of something bigger (the four levels of HR excellence) and all the actions I have taken throughout the past year were consistent with that model.

So, I am summarising the Kirkpatrick's model just for you to have an idea about it and I'll leave the rest for you on how to know more about it, you could read Kirkpatrick's famous book, *Evaluating Training Programs*, as I did. The model consists of four stages[3]:

1. The reaction stage. in this stage Kirkpatrick reemphasised the importance of capturing the people's feedback in a training context about how they approached the trainer and the training. This feedback is gathered through a feedback sheet that includes key questions like asking how do you see the presentation skills of the trainer, usually there is a numerical scale (e.g. 1 – 4) that corresponds with each statement. Kirkpatrick's highlights although this stage doesn't yield a lot of valuable information (e.g. the evaluation at this stage could be built upon subjective opinions) but it's important to the degree that if the feedback from trainees was not positive it will affect the subsequent stages.

---

[3] Evaluating Training Programs, Donald L. Kirkpatrick and James D. Kirkpatrick 2006. The Four Levels: An Overview.

2. The second stage is the learning stage and here your purpose as an HR professional is to make sure that the intended purpose of the training and which is building a new knowledge base and to convey a new learning to the employees has taken place. Usually most of the actions at this level starts from doing a pre-test for the people who went through a training course in order to capture their learning level and most importantly is to do a post-test after finishing the course in order to know if the learning level for the employees has increased. This level is very important if you want to move to the next stage (the behaviour) and if you want to succeed at converting the learning into concrete actions.
3. Behaviour change or transfer to learning is the third stage and here begins the real challenge for any HR or training professional. Throughout this stage you need to make sure that the learning (whether soft skill or hard skills) that happened is converted successfully to the workplace. The direct managers play a key role to make this happen. They are the drivers for any change so if a proper concern and follow up is being exerted from the HR and the direct manager you can guarantee that the learning will be conveyed successfully to the workplace. Usually a clear system of KPIs that relate to the new training can help facilitate behaviour change or the transfer to the job.
4. The final stage is the results, this stage is the most difficult and its difficulty comes from the lack of information or data that relates to any new training initiative. It's easy as we said to capture the employees' feedback or reaction at the first stage because the source of this data or information are the employees themselves while it becomes more difficult at this level because the source of data doesn't lie in one area, it's mostly spread over many places. Let's say that you have trained your production workers on how optimise the usage of the resources available or the raw material they have in order to decrease the waste and to increase the productivity, how you can prove that your training has proven successful? Going through the first three stages is not difficult but when you reach the final stage how you will measure your results. Here you need to prove that what has been done has affected the profit margin of the organisation positively. This won't be easy because you need to gather information from the supply chain department on whether the raw material orders have decreased because of the new training intuitive. If yes, you need to verify that achievement financially through the finance department. You need to double check in the first place if the saving in waste was a real effort from the production worker not because the supply chain department has brought new logistics sources with lower prices. But although it's very difficult to gather and to validate information at the final level the value that this level brings is so high and will help us as an HR or training professionals to justify the training dollars and will definitely enhance our credibility in the organisation.

Training management is a very critical function in any organisation. Many organisations are now paying attention to how much the training is vital to their success, they are investing more dollars in training their employees than before even in the hard times when the economy was down. The financial crisis that hit the world in 2008 had its effects on most organisations all over the world, companies have realised how weak they were after the crisis. They were in trouble trying to recover from that crisis while trying to enhance their financial situation.

The problem was evident and it lied internally in the organisations' workforce abilities. So, the opportunity was so magnificent for those who took advantage of it. The companies that invested in reshaping their wellbeing through training and development during the crisis were able to stand up again and to move quickly after things got better. Those who didn't take advantage of the opportunity were doomed to fail.

Training if managed properly is going to be a safe net for you and your organisation in good and bad times. It's the driver to achieve more excellence in our organisations, it's the key to have a satisfied customer through a well-offered service. So, it's up to you whether you wanted to thrive in these difficult times or not, the answer is more training and training and training.

Performance Management Essentials

Creating a Culture of Star Performers

Peter Senge in his book *The Fifth Discipline* talked about the learning organisation. The organisation that has the ability to adapt to the changes in its environment quickly and effectively. He established his theory based on five factors. Personal mastery was one of these factors. This factor states that organisations that have the ability to create a culture where people are committed to self-learning will create a competitive advantage that will help them to thrive in their environments and to sustain their existence for the long run.

This principle should be the basis upon which each organisation should build their performance management systems around. The issue of managing the employee performance and thus the organisational performance has been a big issue and a lot of debate has been around for decades about the best approach to manage the employee performance. Is managing performance a process of two-way communication (the manager and the employee)? Is it a two-way process that occurs occasionally or continuously? Is it a process that involves many parties other than the employee and the manager? What is it about?

Managing the employee performance is much bigger than all the previous elements that I've just mentioned. It could be all these elements gathered to each other. It could be every one of these elements in addition to other elements (e.g. two-way process + third party validation). Regardless of the way that the organisation is following through to manage their employees' performance there is one major element that these organisations must have.

The focus of all of these approaches is one major issue, **to develop the employee capacity through a well-thought out and deliberate approach that aims to enable the employee to work individually and collectively with others in order to create a state of self-dependency through which the employee can progresses throughout his/her career autonomously**.

Let's now break down this statement to its elements in order to understand more what does it mean and how it affects creating the culture that we aspire to have. The essence of any performance management system is represented in the first part of the statement **(to develop the employee capacity)**. If these systems are not being deployed properly then they will not achieve the intended goal of broadening the employee capacity to handle his/her tasks properly and then to go higher in the task scale in order to handle more advance tasks.

Any performance management system that tracks only the employee's activities during a timeframe and is not focusing on the strategic part of the system that we just mentioned is not a proper system and will create more hurdles than solutions and eventually will not create the star performers culture.

The second part of the statement (through a well-thought out and deliberate approach) focuses on the importance of designing comprehensive learning plan for the employee that includes both the technical and behavioural sides of the employee's job. The gap that exists in many performance management systems when it comes to learning plans is the disconnect between the employees learning plan and the real requirements and behaviours needed on the job.

I have seen many performance management systems that have these two elements (the behavioural and the technical) in its composition but the value they bring to the system is not so high. The first part (the behavioural) should be linked mainly to the company values and if your system is not aligned with these values then you will not move your workforce into the right direction, like if your system is focusing on the business sustainably as one of your core values but the system doesn't include detailed behaviours or indicators that constitute a roadmap to the employees on how to do business in way that sustains it in the long term.

Also, if your technical part if the system that relates to the job is not linked to the real requirements of the job then this will widen the gap and will create a vacuum in the company that will prevent it from reaching its hard goals. Most of the performance management system focuses on a subjective evaluation for the employees' job without having a clear and quantifiable measures that base the evaluation process on a clear criterion. Performance management systems that lack a clear framework of KPIs as related to the technical side of the system will be a hindrance to the organisational excellence and thus improving the overall performance.

To enable the employee to work individually and collectively with others in order to create a state of self-dependency is the third part of our definition. The essence of this statement is to enable the employee through the previous two steps to work on his/her weaknesses by relying on himself/herself individually. The goal is to distribute the burden of the learning process from the employer to be equally shared between the employee and the employer. Historically the principle that was prevalent is that the employee should be guided throughout his/her career without holding any responsibility on whether he/she has to pursue his/her own development.

This principle has changed and even it has been eliminated in some cases. In global and large organisations where there is a big number of employees the issue of following up the employee's career plans individually is nearly impossible. The systems in these companies tend to be more bureaucratic so if the employee didn't do the necessary actions in order to be develop him/herself then there is a big possibility that the employee won't have an opportunity to advance. So, it has become very vital that the employee is the architect of his/her own development plan.

But what about the word **Collectively** as we just said that the employee must be held accountable against his/her own development. Here I mean to have a culture where the employee can refer to a coach, mentor or colleague when he/she is in need of support or help, it's impossible that the employee can depend solely on him/herself when it comes to career advancement. There should be a certain level of support when it comes to personal development plans but it shouldn't be a trend or a norm, it should be an exception.

The last part of the definition **through which the employee can progresses throughout his/her career autonomously** is a reaffirmation that the employee through the previous actions must be enabled and empowered in order for him or her to excel in the career progress journey independently. Organisations that focus and invest heavily in their employee's development and coaching are in a better place to achieve their goals and to sustain their existence in the long run. Within this concept I will highlight on the coaching concept.

There is a misunderstanding between big numbers of managers on how to deliver coaching. There are portions of mangers who believe that coaching is about telling the employee what must be done in a detailed way so no mistakes or gaps would happen. This is not coaching; it's about giving directions to your employees so they would be able to follow through your steps. But the big problem is that they will come back to you every time they face a problem. Coaching is not about doing that at all.

The right coaching is about enabling your employees to solve their problems on their own. The right approach and techniques you need to use for a proper coaching technique is not a topic we will cover here, but my major advice to you when it comes to coaching is to use questioning as a major technique that will open a new possibility for the employee to discover. You need within this context to ask the employee the right questions when they are seeking your help. You need to make them think through a situation so they can find the solutions by themselves.

If the employee asked you as their manager to tell them about the solution for a severe conflict that happened between a manager and his employee. The first question to ask here is the following, how the conflict reached to that degree in the first place? By asking this open-ended question you are intriguing your employee to explore and to investigate the reasons that caused the conflict to reach to that degree which will force them to gather the needed information about the conflict which will help them to understand the triggers for the conflict.

In a subsequent stage you will ask other open-ended questions that will help the employee to reach the solution. But the key idea is the following, it's more effective to follow this approach rather than to ask yourself about the reasons for the conflict. By following the latter approach, you will be inclined unconsciously to give the answers for the employee and this would be against the effective

approach of coaching your employee so that they would be able to figure out the solutions by themselves.

Creating a culture of self-learning in any organisation is a hard work and it requires a deliberate and consistent follow up. A follow up on how employees are moving in their annual learning plans, it's about taking corrective actions when your employees are stuck in their careers and they don't know where and how to navigate the right career choices. It's about spending time with your employees and empowering them to take their daily work decisions that will ultimately contribute to more excellence and self-motivation to do more.

All what I have mentioned till now in addition to the senior management support for learning strategies will contribute largely to create a culture of star performers that will enable any organisation to achieve its goals.

Performance Management System Framework

Performance management as a key function and part of the four levels of HR excellence comes under the human capital category and is classified within the second level of the model (The Intermediate HR). This function is one of the most important ones in HR, it's the driver and the catalyst for the training and development function. I've mentioned before that training your employees without the link to an effective performance management system will not yield the intended result compared to having the training and development function as a natural outcome of the performance management system.

In the first case the training and development needs are not targeted neither they are competency based, while in the second one the training and development function is targeted to enhance a specific job competency. Performance management as a function serves also as the infrastructure for the level above which is the advance level that targets the succession management function. Many companies are struggling to reach that level.

The reason is neither the lack of talent (although finding and nurturing talent is becoming more difficult) nor the lack of the organisational resources to develop the talent. It's mainly the gaps in the performance management systems or in some cases the absence of these systems (I will cover that aspect in the next chapter).

Performance management systems usually follow a common path and it is depicted in the below model below.

Figure 26 – The Performance Management Path

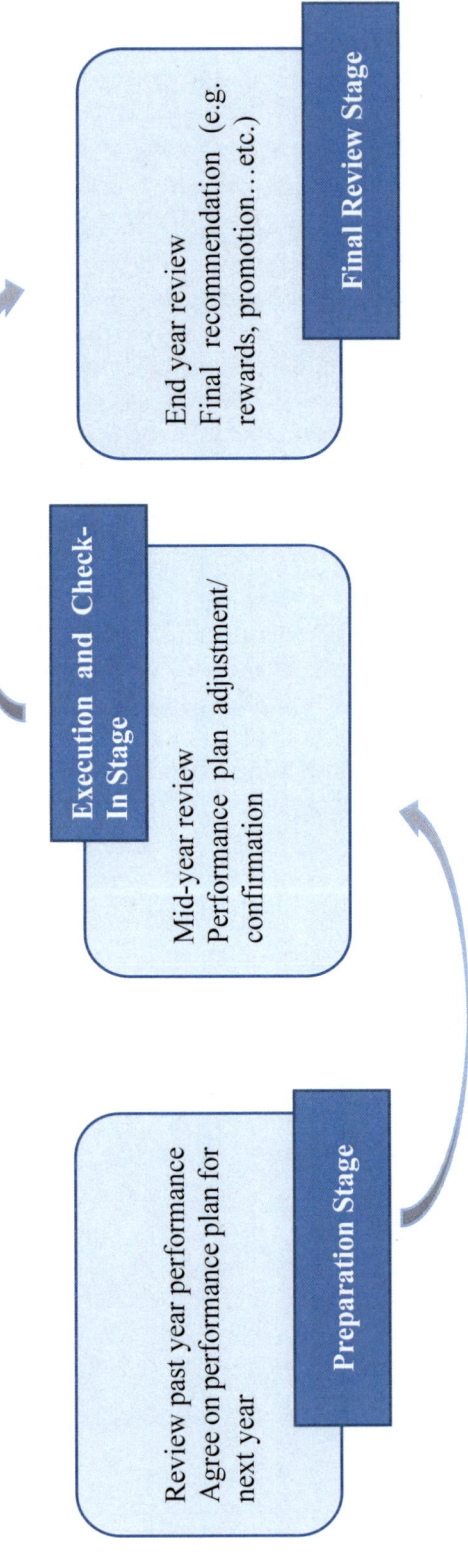

The First Stage (The Preparation Stage) is concerned with laying out a proper foundation through which the employee and the manager can start from toward making a realistic and effective learning plan that the employee can embrace confidently in order to develop the employee's performance. Usually this stage consists of two phases:

1. **Review past year performance.**
2. **Agree on performance plan for next year.**

Before starting the first phase the roles and responsibilities of the key stakeholders in the organisation regarding the performance management system must be clear and spelled out at the beginning of the process. This would eliminate any misunderstanding that could happen later on in the process. Usually the people involved in this process are the employee, the direct manager of the employee and the human resources representative. The roles and the responsibilities of these stakeholders are illustrated below.

The employee has the following responsibilities:

- Agree on the individual objectives based on the department goals.
- Clarify overall career goals and prepare a development plan.
- Assess (self-assessment) their progress, and find ways to overcome obstacles.
- Deliver on their objectives and development plan.

The manager has the following responsibilities:

- Ensure employees understand how their jobs fit into "the big picture."
- Jointly set annual performance objectives with employees.
- Support employees.
- Recognise their progress and their achievements.
- Ensure that performance review is complete and submitted to the HR department.
- Ensure the process is administered fairly and equitably.
- Have a focus for making the process an important part of the company's performance excellence plan.

The HR representative has the following responsibilities:

- Maintain the integrity of the process.
- Provide assistance to managers and employees throughout the process.
- Regularly monitor and evaluate the process.
- Produce and circulate KPIs for the business.

Of these responsibilities there are two key roles. The first one is for the manager and specifically ensuring that the employee understand the importance of his role. Most of the individual learning plans that the mangers carry out for their employees fails not because they aren't well designed and crafted but because the employee doesn't feel the ownership of the plan. This feeling is one of many reasons that could hinder the advancement of any learning plan, but one of the most important reasons is the lack of the employee's understanding about how his/her job fits with the overall picture of the organisation.

In other words, the employee is not able to see the connection between her job and the organisation's major direction. The manager here plays a vital role. The manger must invest the time and effort needed in order to show the employee how valuable his work to the organisation is. The issue is not so complex as somebody could think so. I remember a case that happened with me when I was working with an ex-employer.

I was overseeing a technical training department that had a supervisor and two technical trainers. One of the trainers was a newly graduated person and his main task in the first three months was to make sure that the technical assessments conducted for the technicians who applied to the company was carried out right and effectively. After two months this junior trainer submitted his resignation. When I asked his supervisor about the reason for that resignation, he said that the trainer felt undermined because of doing the technical assessments and it was taking a big portion of his time.

I remember how I was pissed off, not because of the trainer's resignation but because of the supervisor's confirmation that this task is mundane. I asked the supervisor a question. What do you think the result would be if the trainer didn't discover the technician's technical aptitude and, a hiring decision was taken? At this moment the trainer stopped for a moment and then he smiled. At that point I knew that he understood the message, the message that I guaranteed to be delivered to the trainer.

The supervisor in this situation failed to recognise the fact that the industry we were working in is very sensitive and complicated. A technician who is not a technical right fit could cost the company a lot of money when making mistakes. It's not a bank reconciliation that you made and didn't match your books. In our situation a technician who is not technically competent could make a repair that is not congruent with the technical standards and thus could cost the organisation thousands of dollars. I have witnessed personally many cases during my tenure with that employer.

There is a thin line between linking the value of a job to the organisation's mission and failing to do so. The issue is about building the systems thinking skill that any manager must have. This skill is about understanding the organisational functions and their components and how to see them all as a complete one body. By building that skill you will be able to examine all the details related to any job and to link them directly with the organisational strategy and how these jobs can add value to the organisation. Most of the underestimation that the employees are facing comes from the absence of this link. I am highlighting in this issue because it's very important and a lot of the elements in the performance management system would be built upon it.

Now let's get back to the first point in **The Preparation Stage (Review Past Year Performance)**. This stage is applicable to organisations that have current performance management systems in place. For companies that are applying the system for the first time this step would be applicable after completing a cycle of the process (usually one year). This stage is usually conducted in the timeframe from December to January. The goal behind that timeframe is to allow the manger and the employee to review the employee's current performance and to prepare for next year performance.

At this stage there are some actions that must be conducted from both the employee and the manager. Through this review the manager should review the employee's job performance including the **Results** that the employee has achieved (the objectives as represented in KPIs) and the **Behaviours** (as related to the values of the company) that the employee demonstrated during the review timeframe. The goal is to make sure that the employee has achieved her goals successfully and if not, to know the reasons that prevented her from achieving these goals and how to overcome them for the next period.

The second point in the **Preparation Stage (Agree on Performance Plan for Next Year)** the manager and the employee will agree on the performance plan (including the objectives and the behaviours required from the employee) for the next year. Usually this step is being conducted in the timeframe from December to January as for the previous step. During this step the manager should focus on having an open discussion with the employee for the purpose of reaching an agreement on how the employee has performed and what are the objectives for the next period.

Below are the guidelines and the stages that the manager and the employee should follow when conducting performance review **(Preparation Stage – Agree on Performance Plan for Next Year)** in order to contribute to an effective session and thus an effective outcome. They are the following:

1. Planning and preparing for the review, and here the manger should make sure that the place where they are conducting the review is quiet and that the interruptions are to the minimum. The manager should allow enough time for the employee (one-week notice) to prepare for the review, and you need to clarify the objectives of the meetings beforehand. The manger is requested also to prepare carefully by identifying the discussion points before the review like listing the examples of the demonstrated performance from the employee during the past period.
2. The structure and the content of the discussion. Here the manager must establish a relaxing climate that puts the employee at ease. The manager should set from the start the structure of the discussion, the duration of the discussion and how it will go. Also the manager must tell the employee about what will happen later on after the review. After that the manager should begin the discussion and here the main target is for the manager to navigate the achievements of the employee and the difficulties faced during the evaluation period. The end result is a

summary that should be agreed upon between the employee and the manager which will constitute the base for next year's performance plan.

During this session and the related conversation, the manager should follow some important rules that will result in an effective dialogue or coaching session:

* It's recommended that the manager should use certain type of questions that will contribute to the effectiveness of the conversation. Open-ended questions that begin with how, what, why, where, when, tell me about are a key example of the questions that must be used in a performance review session. Closed questions that require a yes or no answer are also helpful when you want to control the flow of information. Sometimes you need to ask a leading question in order to reach a consensus in a certain matter or a conformation on a business fact from the employee but these questions should be kept to the minimum level otherwise you will dominate the discussion. The best approach is to use a blended approach that gathers all the above elements as per the situation.
* The second important thing that the manager should focus on is how he/she is an active listener. This skill is very important and it could be even a vital skill that would make or break a conversation. Sometimes the failure of a coaching or performance review conversation is attributed mainly to the manager's bad listening skills and not to other reasons like his/her inability to direct a conversation or a review session. In order for the manager to be an effective listener the following approach must be followed through. **Active Listening** comprises the following elements:
- Look interested: when you go through a conversation with your employee you should look interested. This means to show the employee genuine interest in meeting him and listening to his problems carefully with a genuine interest to solve the problem. Any sign of indifference to the employee's problem and conversation like looking at your laptop frequently while talking with the employee will result in negative consequences that will affect the whole process.
- Involve yourself by responding: here the manager must acknowledge the emotions coming out from the employee during the conversation. If the employee was experiencing a tough year because of the illness of her husband which affected her performance you need here to acknowledge the fact the reason behind the bad performance was due to the employee's private condition. Suppose that the employee has kept a continuous record of exemplary performance during the past years. Doing this will facilitate the whole process because you have responded to the employee's emotional state which will make the employee grateful for this response, it's a human nature to value people who value us.

- Stay on target: the manager must keep their focus on maintaining the course of the conversation on the right track. Navigating other irrelated topics will result in a divergence from the key topic which is reviewing the employee's performance and doing that could give a signal to the employee that you are trying to manoeuvre the whole conversation and will yield negative results.
- Test your understanding: you need here to make sure that the message you have received from the employee is clear and that you didn't miss any important element during the conversation. To restate the facts said during the conversation from both parties is an effective approach to guarantee that everything is on track, you could also ask the employee to send an email with all the points in the conversation as a reaffirmation of what has been said during the session.
- Evaluate the message: here you need to look at the message from a broader perspective. It's not enough only to restate what have been said. It's most important to identify whether the message is in alignment with the overall goal or objective of the conversation. If you are going through a one-on-one conversation and the employee told you at the end of the session that they will be expecting a promotion by the year end, then you must be careful to realign the employee again with the major goal of the conversation and which is to develop the employee capacity in order for them to be able to occupy advance positions in the future. So, the employee's development is linked with achieving certain goals, by doing that you will guarantee an effective message evaluation.
- Neutralise your feelings: this is the most important step you could ever face when doing a one-on-one review. It's part of our inherent psychological shortcomings to judge people without realising that we are doing that or how much it's affecting the effectiveness of the two-way communication (The essence of the one-on-one session) between the manger and the employee. This judgement is normally affected by many factors, one of these factors is the halo/horn effect. Here the manager tends to judge the person according to a major strength or weakness the employee had in the past and to continue making the same judgement regardless if the employee didn't acquire new skills or even if they has beaten an old negative trait they was suffering from. Such judgment will definitely shadow the session and will cause negative consequences. Unless we develop a high level of discipline so we can control such emotions then we will not deliver an effective review session and a considerable level of communication noise will dominate the session.

3. The review process itself. Here begins the actual performance review and the evaluation of the employee. The manager will focus their attention on major two outcomes, the behavioural and the technical. At the technical side of the process the manager will measure the

employee's performance as related to his/her job description while at the behavioural side the manager will measure how much the employee is aligning their behaviour with the company's core values. After conducting this review, the manager must document the findings so they would be kept for future reference.
4. Objective and development plan. This this the final stage through which the objectives and the development plan is being assigned to the employee. This stage is the end result and the outcome of the previous three stages. At this stage the manager and the employee must jointly assign the training plan that will enable the employee to achieve their goals in order to meet the assigned objectives.

The second stage is the Execution and the Check-In Stage. This stage is comprised of two parts:

1. **Mid-year review.**
2. **Performance plan adjustment/conformation.**

At the first part you make a formal review of the accomplishments achieved by the employee, you review the goals assigned to the employee in the learning plan, you double check on the competency development plan, you ask the employee if additional resources are required to move forward the goals achievement process in addition to any concerns that the employee has faced during the course of his learning plan. What I have said till now doesn't mean that the manager shouldn't review the employee's performance continually. On the contrary to that, the manager must continuously follow up on the employee's learning action plan and to support them so they would be able to achieve their goals.

At the second part you agree with the employee on any changes made to the plan or the plan would be confirmed again and the employee continues moving forward to achieve their goals. The benefit of such a meeting is to give a fair chance for the employee so he/she would be able to defend any proposed changes to the plan. The world we live in today is highly volatile and unpredictable so sometimes you might need to adjust some of the goals in your employees' learning plan to reflect the external environment. By doing that you guarantee the needed alignment between the employees' goal and the organisational goals.

The third and the final stage is the final review stage. At this stage you need to do the following:

1. **End year review.**
2. **Final recommendation (e.g. rewards, promotion…etc.).**

The year-end review is dedicated for the manager and the employee to make a comprehensive evaluation regarding whether if the employee has achieved the annual goals as per her learning plan. The manager would apply the ranking score applicable in the organisation and make the final recommendations for the employee like if the employee has made remarkable achievement then the manager would recommend to grant the employee a big financial bonus and a training program to be rolled out the year after.

Now I will highlight on a sample performance review form that will help you to start the process in a systematic and efficient way and I will highlight on the shortcomings of using an evaluation scale and how to beat it. But before that I will mention below some points that you should pay attention to in order to guarantee an effective performance review:

1. HR must play a key role to guarantee that the review meetings conducted by managers are fair and to reflect the purpose of the performance management system in the organisation.
2. A feedback loop should be created in the system from the beginning in order for the HR to gather information about how the system is being applied. HR must collect feedback regarding if the system has achieved its intended results. Also of the key issues to ask about is to examine any shortcomings in the system that might hinder the future success of the system.
3. One of the most important steps in addition to creating a safe harbour for the employees is to help the managers to prepare for a better performance review by showing them how to conduct a competency-based review that is as much as possible far away from the personal bias.
4. HR has also the ultimate responsibility to make sure that the performance management system is aligned with the organisational objectives and mission. This task is very difficult but if HR has built a credibility within the organisation then this mission becomes easier. Your role here as an HR professional is to make an audit check at the last quarter of the year in order to see if the individual goals are aligning with the overall goal of the organisation. If for example one of the organisational goals is to increase the efficiency ratio of the production lines in your organisation then you must guarantee that the goals at the individual level reflect that goal. Increasing the operational excellence competence for the production staff as a goal that is dictated from the production manager won't bring operational benefits as much like making job rotation as the major strategy for the first level staff. Operational excellence could be a competency for higher level personnel.

These steps are key in order for your performance management system to work effectively into action. Now I will preview a sample performance review form that you can build on as model that can help you when you build your own performance review form.

This form is intended to show you how the dynamic elements of the performance management system are all gathered into one document so it would be easier for both the manager and the employee to track the progress of the system.

Figure 27 – The Performance Review Form

One to One: Performance Review

Review Year

Employee Name: Employee Number:
Job Title: Branch/ Location:

Section 1: Performance in the Role

Core Job Performance	1	2	3	4	5	Overall Comments
Performance against job responsibilities						

Competency Demonstration	1	2	3	4	5	Overall Comments
Teamwork						
Innovation						
Customer service						
Drive						

Please Detail Any Other Areas of Performance/Significant Achievements Which Should Be Noted

1 = Unsatisfactory 2 = Not Fully Achieved 3 = Valued Performer 4 = Excellent 5 = Outstanding

Section 2: Achievement Against Specific Objectives

	Mid-Year Review Comments	**Mid-Year Review Comments**
Objective 1:		
Objective 2:		
Objective 3:		

Section 3: Action Plan

Career Aspirations:

Action Required	Details	Date to Be Completed By	Notes

Section 4: Manager's Overall Assessment

How would you rate the employee's overall performance over the last 12 months?					
Outstanding		Valued Performer		Unsatisfactory	
Excellent		Not Fully Achieved		Other	
Manager's Comments:					
Final Recommendations:					

Section 5: Employee Comments on Performance Review:

Comments:

Section 6: Line Management Support

How do you rate the support of your line manager/supervisor over the last 12 months?							
Very Supportive		Supportive		More Support Preferred		Little Support	
Employee Comments:								

Section 7: General Manager Comments

Comments

Employee:…………………………… Date………………..

Manager/Supervisor:…………………. Date……………….

General /Manager:……………………. Date……………….

Section no. 1 deals with the evaluation process itself. Here the manager has a burden to evaluate the employee against two major parts, the job description and the competency part. In the first part the manager mostly will rely on the KPIs (Key Performance Indicators) assigned to the employee in order to have a quantifiable evaluation for the employee that shows how she/he has done regarding achieving the assigned KPIs. Assigning and designing a related and realistic performance indicator is a very sensitive and complex task that needs both KPIs design technical expertise and business acumen.

HR professionals who are able to design KPIs but don't have the business acumen competency will suffer making objective KPIs and their relatedness to the organisational strategic goals is weak. HR professionals who have the business acumen competency but lack or have weakness in the KPI's technical design will yield qualitative rather than quantitative KPIs which will contribute to widening the gap between the organisational leaders' aspirations and the actions implemented on the ground. It's required to have both, the technical expertise and the business acumen.

In the second part the manager will make the evaluation against the competencies that are required to be exhibited from the employees. Here I am talking specifically about the behavioural side of the performance review that is taken from the core values of the organisation. The evaluation process here must be based on identifying the standards per each value or competency, like if we said that customer service is a core value for our company then we must explain in more detail how this value will be translated into behavioural standards (e.g. taking responsibility for solving customer-service problems within responsibility level).

Also, one of the most important things is to a have clear scoring system for both sides of the evaluation process. In other words, the KPIs for every job must be given a weight and that weight must be converted into a scoring system that could be a scale from $1 - 5$. The same thing applies to the behavioural part of the evaluation process. You need to give every behavioural standard a weight that must be translated also into scoring system. Suppose that you have tested the validation of your scoring system, then you will be able to quantify the evaluation process by assigning the employee the corresponding score and thus minimising to a large extent the subjectivity in assigning the scores.

A key issue that must be highlighted here is the human factor in the evaluation process. Regardless of the scoring system you have used the subjectivity in the evaluation process will still have an effect, but by designing quantifiable standards the subjectivity in making the judgement will be at a minimal degree. It's completely a different case to say to your employee that her score was four according to the scoring system without any justification or to tell her that the score she had was given to her because she didn't meet some standards as assigned in the evaluation process. In both ways you are making a judgement but the degree of the subjectivity in the second case is much less than the first one.

At the end of section 1 the manager can write in more detail about the achievements the employee has achieved. Here you are giving your managers more room to expand on the evaluation process itself. You don't want to end up with a rigid evaluation score that quantify the human behaviour in figures and facts only. Writing about how the employee has achieved his goals like if the employee has exhibited extraordinary team spirit that enabled the team to achieve a major goal would encourage the employee to do more in the future. It also reflects a realistic picture about how the employee has achieved his goals which will contribute to a fairer evolution system and thus rooting the new behaviours exhibited by the employee as the new norm in the organisation.

At section 2 you assign the objectives that the employee must achieve for the upcoming period. These objectives are the end result of the outcome of section 1. The essence of the evaluation process is not only to make a judgement about how the employee has done in the past. The major goal of the evaluation process within the broader context of managing performance is to know the areas of improvement per each employee and in turn to assign the relevant developmental goals that will stretch the employee's performance and potential.

The process of assigning developmental goals should be a two-way communication process through which the employee contributes effectively in making her goals. The key rule is that employees will hold themselves accountable if they participated in making their goals. Goals design and preparation is out of our scope in this book. But it's worth mentioning that the SMART rule to design the performance objectives should be followed here. Also, another important consideration is to give the employee a room to apply the goals in their own terms, employees will achieve their goals if they believe they have control over their achievement.

Employees are encouraged also to add their input regarding their aspirations within Section 3. The idea here is to motivate the employee to move to higher stages within the organisational echelons. Employee will achieve more than they are required to do if they believe that they will excel at the organisation they work for. At this section also the objectives set in the previous section should be translated into action plans. Some goals could be tackled through training needs fulfilment, other goals could be met through coaching. The process of goal setting is not complete and effective unless you support it with the proper action required to achieve it.

At the end of performance review period which is usually 12 months the manager will make the final evaluation as illustrated in Section 4. Here the manager must decide on the relevant evaluation category that reflects the employee's real performance. The manager will choose a rating criterion that ranges from not fully achieved to outstanding depending on the employee's achievement and the overall performance. The way how you will help your managers to identify the proper rating criterion is dependent on how you are able to quantify the rating criteria or how much you define each criterion in a clear and understandable way. For example, if you have decided that the employee has shown an outstanding performance then you must define the elements of an outstanding performance, you could say that an outstanding performance should include the following:

1. The employee's performance must consistently be of exceptionally high quality.
2. Employees assessed as "Outstanding" stand out clearly from their peer group.

3. Outstanding performers are widely recognised to have achieved very stretching goals and the highest standards in all aspects of their work.
4. They are a role model to others, not only in what they achieve, but also in the manner in which they work.
5. Outstanding performers don't need significant development needs concerning their present job.
6. The development plan for an outstanding performer is directed almost entirely towards the employee's personal development or future career moves.

Such details will help the manager to make an easy and much more objective evaluation. In the final two sections the employee can list any additional information about any areas they wish to add and they can make their evaluation regarding their manager's support throughout the evaluation process.

The last thing that I will mention here is the importance of managing employees' performance from the perspective of coaching them. I will discuss later on in this section the shortcomings of the traditional performance review system and how it affects employees' morale in many cases but still what makes a difference in making your performance management system an effective one regardless of the system's shortcomings is the coaching you deliver to your employees as a key driver of the system.

Coaching your employees should be the norm when trying to deploy a new performance management system. Coaching is about enabling your employees to discover their hidden potential gradually and consistently through self-reliance. If you succeed to do this then you will succeed at your performance management system regardless of its difficulties. You will still have disgruntled employees because of the score they got but at the end of the day if these employees know in heart that their managers are truly effective coaches and that they always do what it takes to develop them then any negative impact your performance management system has will be lessened by the fact that it was designed around a coaching theme.

The Link Between Performance Management and Corporate Strategy

This topic and the rest of the topics in this section will be discussed as key elements that support your performance management system. The idea here is to highlight on some key issues that are complimentary and essential and to make sure that your performance management system is successful.

The first issue here is the link between performance management system and the corporate strategy. We have heard a lot about this issue and how important it is for a successful implementation of the system. Many organisations try to do the needed alignment between their corporate strategy and their performance management system but most of the times they fail to do so. What is the reason behind this failure?

The issue of managing employees' performance is controversial since long time. Company executives are always keen to achieve their business goals through increasing their revenues and market share and these elements are tangible and easy to track and the most important thing is that they happen always during a one-year timeframe which makes them attainable in principle. The issue is the opposite of that when it comes to performance management systems. These systems need a lot of dedication and hard work and time in order to reach an acceptable level of seeing the outcome of the program.

The amount of investment and effort the companies put into such systems compared with the outcome (which is relatively low at the first stages of the system) is not worthy the same amount of time and attention the company executive spends towards different areas of the organisation like managing sales operations. So here starts the problem! How can we expect our management to align their aspirations with a system that is not giving the needed yield? In other cases, the company executives won't even bother asking how the system is progressing into the organisation.

Someone could argue that this issue is not critical to guarantee the success of the system and that by making the needed communication through the executives from the top of the organisation to the lower levels then the alignment will start. My own perspective is that this is true, but it's only the starting point that after it comes many more issues that will help make a successful alignment. Company leaders must follow this communication with one-on-one conversations with the head of departments in order to begin the alignment journey. The head of departments must understand how leaders want to translate their aspirations into concrete actions.

After this issue is settled down the role of the HOD is very critical to make sure that the values are cascaded down to the lowest level in the organisation. Leaders must exhibit the needed values into their day-to-day work so employees would look at them as exemplary leaders that they want to follow. Also, it's important that the HR department plays a key role by translating these values into related standards to make it easy for the managers to track the progress of their subordinates regarding the assimilation of the new behaviours.

Such behaviours and their related standards should be integrated into your performance management system. For example if you are searching for new innovative ways to change your current work structure and their related processes in order to minimise waste and to increase revenue you must make that aspiration very clear in terms of the related behaviours associated with this value. You need to make it clear that the department heads must exhibit many behaviours that encourage innovation like allowing and acknowledging the new ideas coming from their employees.

This issue is the first thing that must be done to make sure that the values of your organisation are cascaded down smoothly into the organisational levels but this also won't help any organisation to guarantee a consistent behaviour change in the organisation. In order to guarantee the consistency in applying the needed behaviours a consistent follow up from HR and the line managers must be a priority. Behaviour change is not easy at all and it takes a lot of effort and time to make that change a reality. Rewarding the exemplary employees who are role models in this behaviour change would contribute to root the new behaviour change.

The issue of behaviour changes and adopting new values that would add up to the culture positively is not impossible. It only takes a dedication from the top management toward making positive changes through behaviour changes and a consistent approach in following up on these changes to make sure that the new changes are institutionalised. HR professionals have also the ultimate responsibility of showing the management how these systems can help the organisation to achieve its goals so management would be encouraged to consider this issue as a vital part of the organisation's main strategy and goals.

The Link Between Performance Management and TR

The second important issue that is integral to the previous one is linking your performance management system with your total rewards system. This doesn't mean just to reward the higher performers and to exclude others. It's about customising the TR elements as per the individual needs of your organisation. A star performer would be rewarded with a generous financial bonus and the employee with the average performance would be rewarded with less than attractive financial bonus but you could add to that a training program for the employee to help them overcome their obstacles and to enable them to reach higher levels in the organisation.

It's a big mistake to steer your total reward system just to a certain portion of the workforce and to exclude others. Of course, the concept of the total rewards is comprehensive and is applicable to all the employees in any company, but the distinguished portion of the workforce receives the most alluring part of the total rewards while others receive the traditional elements that are applicable to everyone regardless of their position or performance like the retirement plans. Your role is to make sure the needed balance in distributing the TR elements fairly. Fairly as I just have stated is to give each and every employee what they deserve as per their individual needs.

TR elements are wide and varied and if managed well can play a vital role in supporting your performance management system. Not all the employees in your organisation are entitled for certain segments of your TR strategy. Each segment in your workforce has its different needs so understanding these needs will help you to align your TR system with your performance management system. X generation is more interested in having a work environment that is based on teamwork, so adjusting the distribution of your workforce to guarantee that your departments are constituted of a proper mix of different generations including Xers would enhance your offerings and will make it easy for them to produce effectively.

It has been proven that linking your performance management system with TR is a recipe for success. Companies invest a lot of time and money into their performance management systems but the failure to make sure that there is a viable link with the TR system would jeopardise the success of such systems. The first point that you must focus on is to reward financially your employees who have been successful in achieving their goals. This point is mostly applicable for companies who are implementing their performance management systems for the first time or are still in the phase of trying the system after completing two or three cycles.

Employees won't be interested to peruse the journey of going through the complexities of performance management unless they see something in the horizon. It's in our nature as human beings to expect a return for anything we are doing whether the return was up to our expectations or not. I remember clearly when I was in charge of deploying a new performance management system in one of the companies I worked for and how the system was stalled for long periods because the management was not sure if they want to reward in a proper way the top performers as a result of applying the system.

There was a big pressure from the department managers about the benefits that the system will bring to the employees other than the development opportunities the employees will be given. They were asking over and over about the outcome that their employees are expecting compared to the effort that they will put during the year. Assigning your employees challenging goals that will extend their potential requires a bog effort from their side so they will expect a return and it's your responsibility to make sure that your performance management system will yield tangible benefits to your organisation and your employees.

Competency-Based Performance Management

Performance management systems are usually geared toward reaching a quantifiable result regarding how and what the employee has achieved through relying on a numerical rating score but as I will explain later this issue creates a lot of conflict between the employee and the organisation which will affect the common interest for both parties. No performance management system is perfect even in organisations that have begun a new era in managing their employees' performance (some companies rely on a two-way communication process that excludes the scoring side of the system), still there will be a problem that won't be eliminated completely. The employee will still feel in both ways that there is only one dominant party (usually the manager) who controls the conversation toward achieving certain goals.

Managing employees' performance should have two dimensions, the first one is favouring the organisation (to achieve the strategic goals of the organisation) while the other is favouring the employee. In this case the focus is to help the employee to achieve his/her career aspirations through the necessary training and development actions. Here comes the role of the competency-based performance management system. Most of the performance management systems have two sides, the first one as we saw in the previous performance review form deals with the job itself while the other deals with the core values of the organisation.

The second part (the core values of the organisation) is applicable to all the employees and is usually easier to administer compared to the first part. Here you assign the values that the employee must exhibit by identifying the performance standards per each value. Although it takes time to develop the performance standards for the core values but overall the process is less time-consuming if we compared it with identifying the performance standards for all the jobs in any organisation. This is the first part of the performance management system.

The main challenge here is to select the most job-related competencies that constitute the critical success factors. Most of the performance management systems fall short because of that side of the process. The difficulty in identifying the job-related competencies and the burden it carries make most of the stakeholders in the process inclined toward routing an easy path. They will try to make the effort to evaluate the employee's performance regardless they had clear performance standards or not.

The issue of designing competencies and their relevant standards is not our topic but the main issue here was to highlight the importance of having clear performance standards that help the manager to base the performance review process upon objective criteria that makes the performance review easier and less subject to conflict and personal judgment.

Performance Rating, Is It Obsolete?

Now the most important thing is for the manager to know how to mitigate the effect of the review session itself. It's well-known that a key disadvantage of the scoring scale of the performance management system is the defence it triggers from the employee when doing the evaluation. It's part of our human nature not to accept the fact that we have been tagged with a numerical score even if that score is high. If you have given your employee a score of 4 out of 5 at the end of their review session then this will make them relatively unsatisfied because they would think that a four score means that they have achieved their goals but the manager is reluctant to give them a five score.

This obstacle has made the performance review session as part of the bigger system of managing performance as one of the most undesired aspects of the system. It's really derailing to go through the complexity of trying to convince the employee that they deserved their score fairly. I believe that the issue of moving to a conversation-based system is a mature step toward achieving a genuine performance change in any organisation but are we ready yet for such a change?

The companies that have reached toward that shift have made so after many years of going through the complexity of what we call the traditional performance management system. The issue here is not to undermine the role this system plays in developing the organisational performance. It's just the problem of scoring the human being whose emotions and behaviours are nearly impossible to quantify. We are not talking about a production line that we can calculate its efficiency. The issue here is much more difficult.

The bottom line is the following, no one organisation can move to the new way of managing their employees' performance unless they experience the complexities of the traditional performance management system. Unless your department heads are competent about how to conduct one-on-one conversation and how to convey criticism in a positive way you will never move to a new era of managing your employees' performance.

Measuring Performance Management System Effectiveness

Measuring performance management system is not an easy task at all. This system is very different and diverse compared to other HR functions in terms of measuring its effectiveness. As we noticed in the previous chapters that most of the HR functions when it comes to measuring their effectiveness have their own specific segments. Recruitment for example has a specific and identified cycle that begins from sourcing reaching to selection and hiring. Training and development also have a specific cycle that starts with TNA and finishes with training delivery.

Measuring the effectiveness of these functions is reachable because they have specific segments that make it easy to track their outcome. You can focus on the key metrics when it comes to recruitment like the time to hire and the cost of hire but if you are approaching the performance management system then the issue is different. Performance management system has many elements that are interacted and related in a way that makes it very hard and inefficient to try measuring all its components.

The first segment in the performance management system is related as we said before to the technical aspects of any job within any organisation. The companies I worked for had an average of fifty unique job titles. Can you imagine how much difficult it is to find a suitable measurement yardstick for these fifty jobs? Even for the general segment of the performance management system (the core values) the issue of measurement is not easy also. Although the core values are applicable to all the employees in the organisation but the way how each department in the organisation impacted the organisation is also very difficult to measure or to quantify.

Someone could argue that all you need is to look at the aggregate results of the performance management system and that is more than enough to decide if the system has achieved its goals. It could be somehow true but can you say that because your overall score in customer service were high that all the departments have the same strengths? Of course not, you need to dig deep in the customer service scores per each department to decide on that. Doing that may seem realistic and may negate that previous premise that going into the details of performance management system is not efficient but I will highlight here that the complexity of going into the details of so many departments and to prove whether the system has achieved its goals or not could put you in the situation of overanalysing where you reach the degree of the analysis paralysis.

The aforementioned is an absolute judgement which means that you can follow this rule in some cases and you can ignore it in others. In smaller organisations that issue of the detailed analysis could be reachable and easy to conduct while in larger organisations the detailed analysis could reach you to nowhere. From my own experience and what I have seen the issue of measuring the performance management system had two sides; the first one was about putting the results you have into suitable and clear graphs that make it easy for any person to know what the overall results were about the other is about measuring the effectiveness of the system through the balanced scorecard model.

I will highlight below some samples about some graphs that reflect the performance evaluation scores for a given organisation.

Figure 28 – Performance Evaluation Scores - Drive Competency

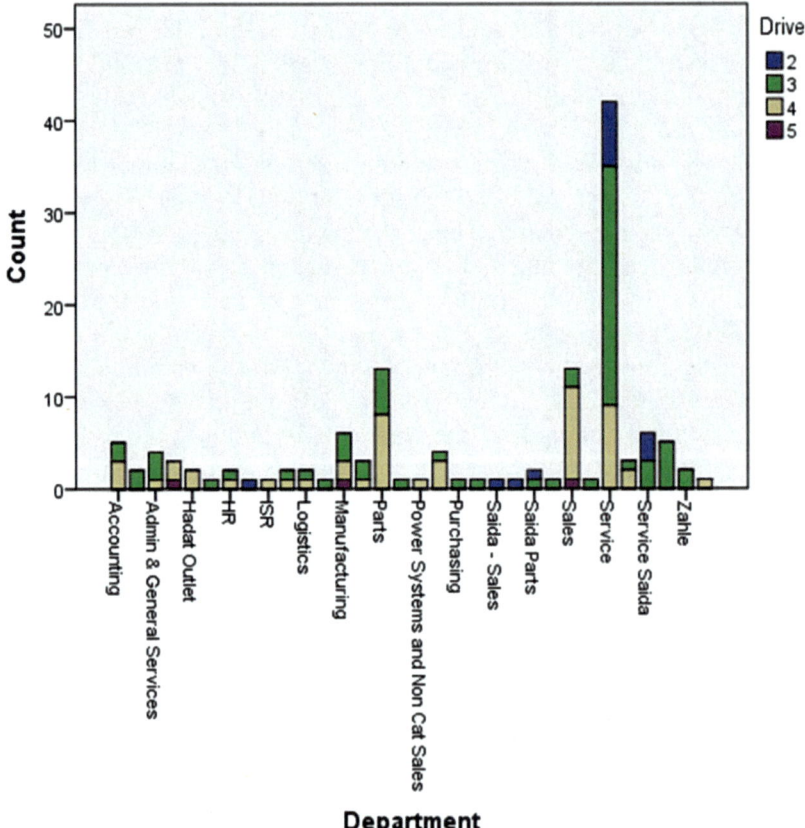

Figure 29 – Performance Evaluation Scores - Teamwork Competency

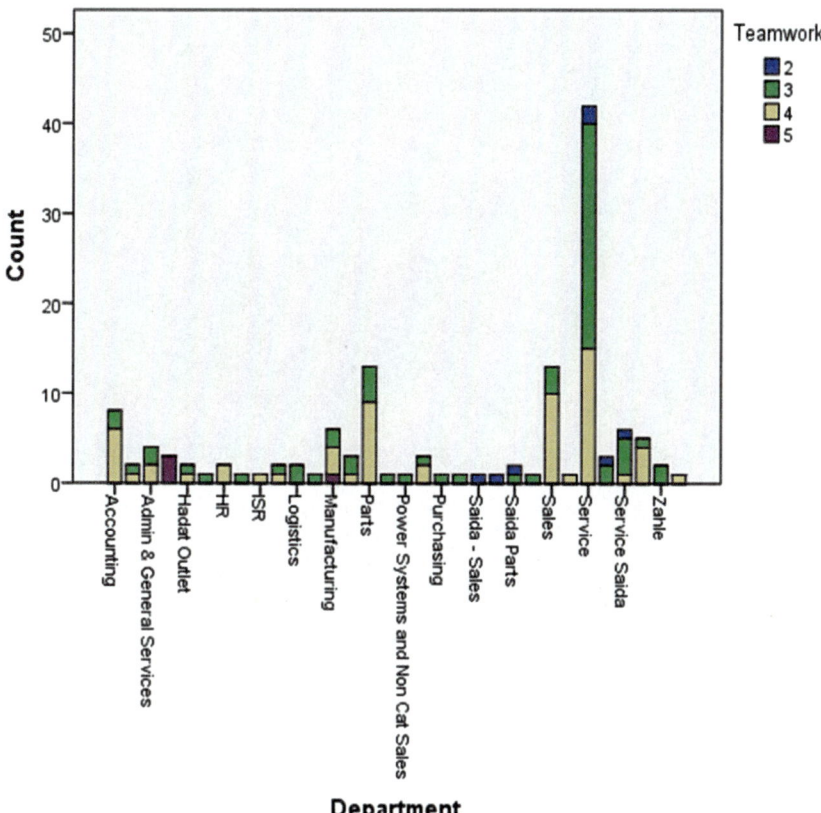

The previous two graphs are an illustration about two core values, Drive and Teamwork, and the graphs represent how each department scored on a scale from 1 – 5. This is the first step toward understanding your overall results.

Before going into the balanced scorecard model and how it relates to performance management system I will highlight on a very important issue. It's about validating your system in terms of the leniency and strictness. For me this was a crucial part as it was important for me to know whether the managers in my organisation were fair in their evaluations. This doesn't mean that they should give high scores neither to give low scores, it's about just being fair.

Most of the performance management systems at least when they are new to the organisation face the problem of leniency or strictness which means that the mangers either would give to a great extent high scores or low scores to their subordinates. These are psychological barriers in our nature as human beings. In order to discover this issue, you need to use the bell curve as a validation tool for this system. The graphs below are an illustration of two organisations with their scores distributed over the bell curve.

Figure 30 – Normal Distribution - Horizon Company

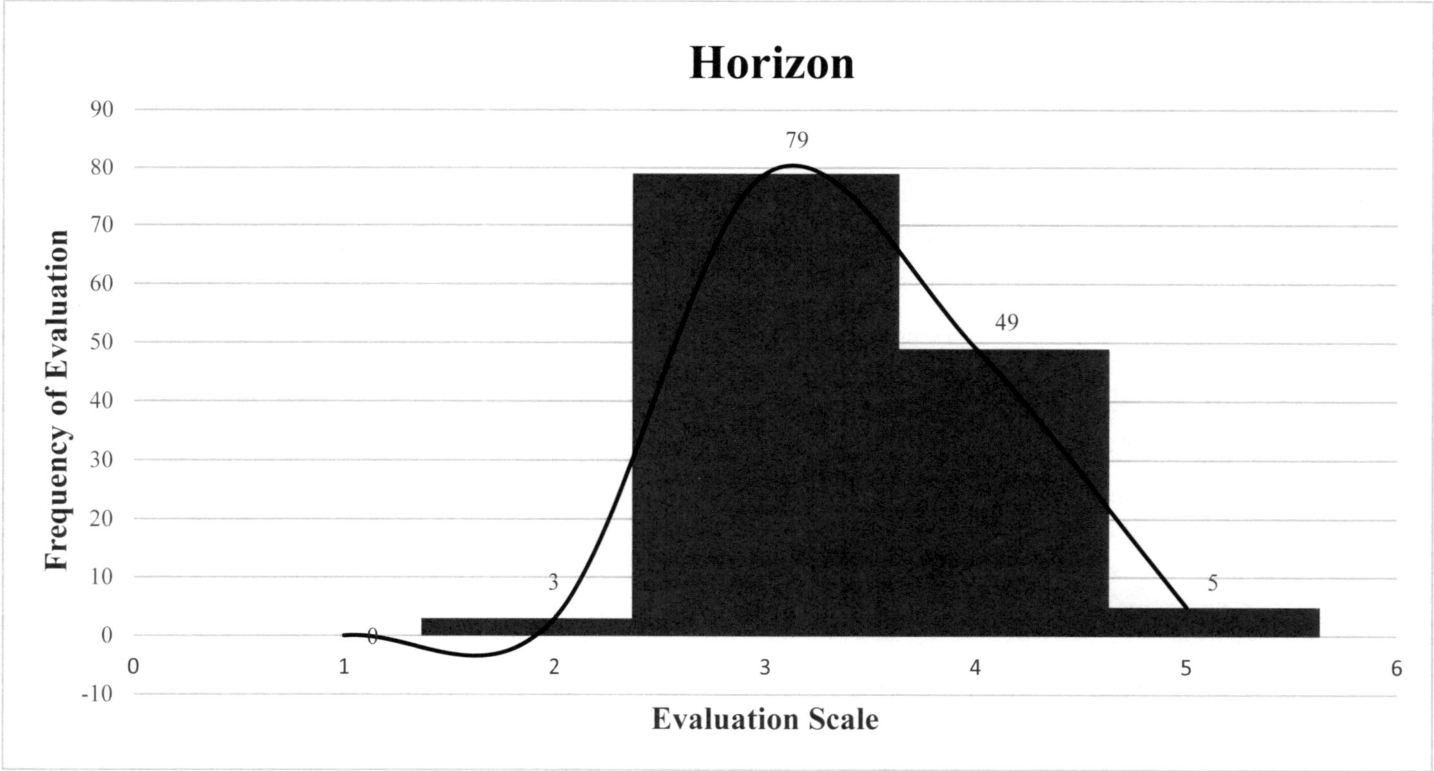

Figure 31 – Normal Distribution - Delta Company

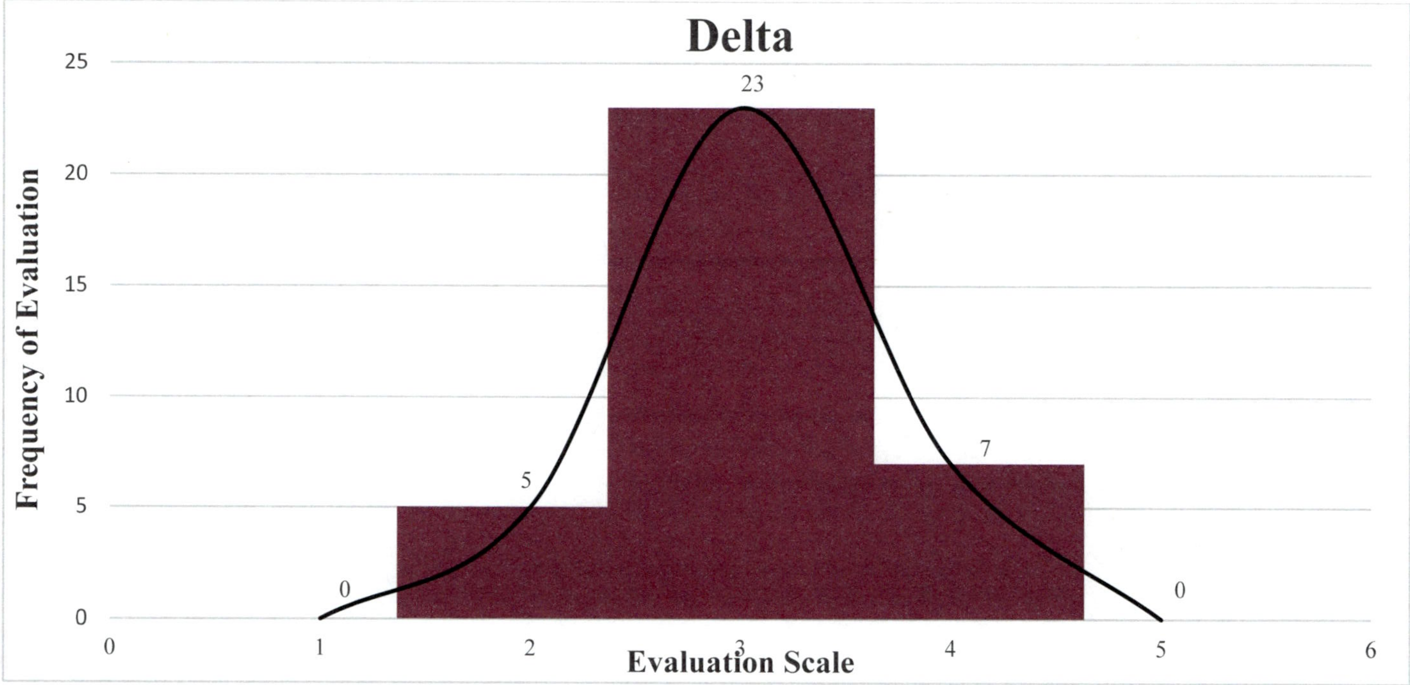

The previous two graphs represent two organisations, Horizon and Delta. The first one shows what we call a skewed bell curve toward the right-hand side. This means that the system is favouring a lot of employees positively which means that most of them were given high scores. There could be cases where the system is skewed toward the left-hand side and in this case the system is putting the employee at the disadvantage of the low evaluation. In the first case the managers most probably are lenient in their evaluations while in the other case they were strict in their evaluations.

Knowing the fact that your managers were lenient or strict in their evaluations gives you the leverage to adjust the system accordingly. In the case of Horizon, you need to make sure that a proper communication has occurred for all the stakeholders and to show them the needed direction and training in order to make sure that in the next evaluation period the direct managers will do a fair evaluation.

The last piece in the performance management measurement is the balanced scorecard model. Within this the performance management system is based against the scorecard model that mainly consists of four elements; Finance, Customers, Processes and Learning and growth. Here you need to examine how the elements of the performance management system are reflected on each segment of the model. Below is a sample of performance management system scorecard.

Performance Management System Scorecards

Performance Management System – Internal Process.

- Performance standards agreed upon for key aspects of the job were clear and quantifiable.
- Performance measurement for key aspects of the job was based upon the agreed job standards.
- Competencies evaluation was based on the standards in the competency appendix.
- Performance objectives were agreed upon properly and mutually.
- Performance objectives were related to the key aspects of the job and the organisational core values.
- Performance objectives were realistic, time-based and action-oriented.
- Performance were integrated with the organisational and departmental objectives.

Performance Management System – Employee Satisfaction.

- Did your manger create the right atmosphere during the performance review session?
- Did the manager discuss the performance related issues or was he/she focusing on your personal traits?
- Has your manager provided feedback throughout the evaluation period as well as during the formal review meetings?
- Did your manager carry out his role as a coach or a counsel during the review period?

Performance Management System – Learning and Growth.

- Did the learning plan set out was effective in terms of its relevance to your training needs?
- Did you learn new skills during the evaluation period?

- Was the learning plan challenging enough that it extended your potential?

The previous questions should be prepared in a survey format that must be distributed to your employee at the end of each review period, the goal is to extract the feedback from the employees regarding how much the system was effective. You should assign a rating scale, let's say from one to four in order to have as much as possible a quantifiable result. The aforementioned factors are examples of questions you can introduce in your scorecard that are relevant to each segment. For example, asking about if the goals were put mutually is an example of how much the manager has followed the guidelines of the performance management process.

As you can notice that the fourth segment of the scorecard wasn't mentioned here. The issue of measuring how the performance management system has impacted financially your organisation is not easy at all. During my experience it was difficult to decide if the performance management system had really a finical impact on the organisation. In some departments especially the revenue generating departments the issue of relating the financial impact of the performance management system to these departments was easier than non-generating revenue departments.

You could choose either to include this segment within your scorecard or not, it depends on your situation and whether if your managers will accept to measure the system without relating it to any financial returns, although this would weaken your overall system effectiveness for the future. A better approach is to start the scorecard with the first three elements without the finance segment and you can include it in future stages once you begin to see an improvement in your overall performance management system outcomes.

The previous model is just a starting point that will help you to put an action plan to improve the system. Although it's a measurement tool but it doesn't give you an answer in what should be done to improve the system. This model will guide you on your priorities and what should be done to enhance the system.

Managing employee performance has been an ever-long struggle, but what should be clear is that improving your employee's performance is the fact that must be embraced by all parties in any organisation. Whatever the means you are using to improve your organisational performance, whether it was through a scoring system or a two-way communication system, what you should target is how to align this side of the development process with the organisational strategies and goals.

Succession Management Essentials

Talent Management

Talent management is the process and actions by which HR professionals focus on sourcing and attracting key talent, integrating key talent within the organisational culture, developing this talent on the highest standards possible and most importantly keeping this talent.

It has been a mistake to follow through the concept of talent management as related only to leaders in higher positions in the organisation. Historically this category of the organisation had the biggest portion of the attention and focus regarding all the employment aspects. Things have changed dramatically in the last few decades and a big shift happened regarding how organisational leaders are now approaching the concept of talent management.

Organisational leaders and HR professionals are now more open to new possibilities and options when it comes to talent management. They are thinking in a more comprehensive perspective regarding their key talent, and when we say key talent, we mean every single employee who has a high potential to be developed for more future opportunities. The concept of talent management has become a comprehensive and integrated process that link all the HR elements and functions toward developing our key talent.

This integration starts from sourcing candidates reaching to the hiring process and beyond that. The goal is to select the most talented candidates who can add more to the organisational value and thus achieving the organisational goals. Also, by selecting the top-notch candidates you can establish and support your leadership pipeline in order to guarantee a continuous succession planning process.

The main reason I have introduced this concept before going to the succession management concepts is my desire to make it clear that the concept of succession management is comprehensive and should include all the employees regardless of their level and by having a robust talent management strategy in place then you will have by default a strong succession management process.

Any inconsistency between your talent management strategy and your succession management process will lead to weak outcomes in terms of creating competent organisational leaders. The ultimate goal here is to have your best talent in place being assigned to the right places in order to serve the organisational goals in a much broader perspective that takes into account the integration of each single step of the talent management strategy in the organisation.

Succession Management Process

The concept of succession management has been developed historically until it reached this current state. Decades ago the concept was about finding the most suitable candidate for the vacant leadership position within the organisation and to fill that position without paying attention to the person who will occupy the position. Here we mean whether the person is in need of development and support or not, this is what we call replacement planning.

The concept was extended into more advance state as dictated by the organisational needs and it was developed into what was called succession planning. Here we still focus on selecting the most suitable candidate for the leadership position but with more careful planning on how to develop that person by designing a proper learning plan that helps the employee to handle the new responsibilities.

This move was an advancement that helped the organisations to retain its best talent and it supported achieving the organisational goals but still there was a problem that was overlooked. By focusing on the key personnel only the organisation lost a big advantage. An advantage to expand its leadership pool from within by including all the employees regardless of their title and more specifically the ones below the managerial level.

In order to cope with these developments and business needs the concept of succession planning was further developed and included all the employees from all the levels in the organisation and by that time the concept was changed to be succession management. So, the bottom line is the following, Succession Management is a concerted effort that targets all the organisational levels with taking into account the individual variations of each employee in order to create a complete chain of successors who are able to occupy a higher-level position in anytime.

In our model at the beginning of the book you can notice that succession management was located at the advance level. This means that this level is not attainable unless you move through the model upward and the same applies for all the levels in the model. In this segment it's ineffective to start your succession management strategy if you don't have an effective performance management system in place. I link this again to the importance of having a comprehensive succession management system that targets the talent in the organisation as a whole.

Performance management system gives you the needed knowledge and awareness of your employees' performance level. This is a prerequisite if you want to locate your most talented employees in order to feed your leadership pipeline fuelled by your succession management strategy. I am highlighting again the idea that this model was based upon. The model starts at the basic level and goes upward, building on the achievements in the previous stages until you reach the top of the model.

Now we will talk about the stages of the succession management process. They are the following:

1. Identify critical jobs. These are the jobs that if left vacant then a big harm would affect the organisation. Most of us would think that these are jobs with a manger or director title but in fact a job doesn't need to be within this category to be classified as a critical job. A highly technical and specialised job that generates a lot of value for the organisation would be considered a critical job. An example of such of job would be an IT Trouble-shooter who is highly capable of solving software related problems. We said before that the concept of succession management extends this effort to include all the levels in the organisation but this doesn't mean that we shouldn't pay close attention to these critical jobs. The goal is to enable the people in these critical jobs to achieve their goals in a very effective and solid manner. The issue of enablement would be easier for lower level jobs in terms of these complexity and development needs, but this doesn't mean that these jobs are not important enough to exclude them from our effort. We said that having a solid performance management system is a key step to build a successful succession management process. Such a system would help to enable employees in lower levels to excel at their jobs.
2. Identify the competencies for these critical jobs. The next step is to identify the development needs of the employees holding these critical jobs according the competencies assigned for these jobs. We talked about how it is important to build job competencies that are relevant to the job and determinant to its success. A specific and targeted development plan is more effective than a general one.
3. Identify high potential employees. Once we have identified the critical jobs and their related competencies the next step is to identify the people who are competent and able to be moved to higher levels in the organisation. Again, I will focus on the importance of having an effective performance management system that would support your efforts in succession management and would help you in identifying the high potentials.
4. Once you have identified the needed competencies for the critical jobs and have identified also the high potential employees you can make a competency-based assessment in order to know the competency level of these high calibre employees. After that comes the preparation of the proper learning plan for these leaders in order to empower them so they can move the organisation to a higher performance level. Then you begin the deployment of this plan with taking into account the needed resources and tools to make it successful.
5. Finally, and after conducting the needed learning plans you make the evaluation for these plans to know if they were able to hit their goal. The evaluation of these plans should be linked to how much these plans were

able to retain the high talented leaders in the organisation and how much these leaders were effective in achieving the organisational goals as measured by their superiors' opinions.

Succession management if played well is an effective recipe for success in any organisation and they are a very effective retention tool that helps any organisation in their retention strategies. This topic is very important but I have decided to write about briefly and very much less than what I have written for the rest of the topics. I have mentioned in one way or another in certain occasions in this book that customisation is required in certain aspects of the model in this book but still the degree of similarity of these functions compared to other functions in other organisations is very high, but the topic of leadership development as part of succession management is very unique. The steps that I've just mentioned about how to create a succession management strategy is the same in any organisation but the methodology of implementation is very unique from one organisation to the other. Even sometimes the methodology if implementation is unique and different from one person to the other.

That's the reason that made me write briefly about the subject as I will leave the implementation sphere to you to decide on. In order to complete the loop for this topic I will talk about some metrics that you can use in order to gauge how effective you are in your succession management strategy and they are listed below.

Measuring Succession Management Systems Effectiveness

Measuring the effectiveness of our succession management systems is needed to the level that can help us to decide whether we have an effective system or not. There are some metrics that we can use to gauge the effectiveness of our succession management systems. They are:

1. Promotion ratio and the total promotions divided by total headcount. The higher the percentage the better.
2. Internal hired ratio, we calculate that metric by having the internal hired divided by total hired. This metric gives you an indication on how much the organisation is focusing on developing and promoting employees from within which will affect your succession management strategy.
3. Succession coverage ratio. This metric is calculated by the number of employees in the successors pool and dividing it by succession applicable positions. This metric is an indication of whether succession plans are effective and taking place in your organisation.
4. Home grown leader's ratio. This metrics shows the number of critical positions in the organisation filled with internal candidates.

The above metrics are helpful in locating your internal talent in the best possible way and give you the advantage of planning ahead of time for your future succession needs.

Conclusion

I wrote at the beginning of this book about how I was approaching the HR strategies in the organisations I worked for based on a trial and error approach. I was planning for my organisation based on its needs but the issue that I overlooked was the absence of a clear model that should have been the guide to a consistent and effective outcome. Tackling training and development needs without linking them to the performance management system was always yielding modest results, I remember how much money we were spending on training initiatives that didn't yield the needed outcome.

In other cases, there was a negative impact on the employees themselves. You can imagine how difficult and demotivating it is to leave your employees without any proper intervention after they finish a training. The employee expects to find the support from both the HR and the direct manager so he/she would be able to apply the new concepts gained from the training. Again, the absence of an interrelated HR model was causing this damage. If I would have been working through the model I introduced at the beginning of this book I would have planned a better way to guarantee an effective outcome from the training the employee attended.

Following through the training segment of the model would have guided me to use the Kirkpatrick model in order to measure the impact of that training. This was an example of the importance of having a clear framework that should guide you when you tackle your HR actions. It doesn't have to be that you use the model in the book as it was reflected. You need just to build on the framework that the model was based upon.

Our world today is facing a lot of uncertainty and ambiguity and this has shed light on our field and it was a big one. We are at the centre of everything happening in our organisations so you need to equip yourself with the competencies needed to succeed in addition to having a robust strategy supported by a clear framework. Having the HR competencies alone without a clear HR model to work thorough will make you the HR expert who can only give advice but can't support it with actions, and having an effective HR model that can guide you to the action to be taken without having the needed HR competencies would give you the leverage to be an action oriented person but would weaken your credibility as the expert who should be able to provide the needed advice.

In order to succeed in this uncertain and ambiguous world you need to have both, the HR competencies and an effective HR framework. It's all about how competent you are to navigate through the complexities of our function and how to turn these complexities into organisational enabled solutions that will add the ultimate value to the business.